MW01708185

DOING BUSINESS WITH THE THAIS

A HANDBOOK FOR EXECUTIVES

Paul Leppert

Patton Pacific Press, Inc.
Sebastopol, California

ASIAN BUSINESS SERIES

THE ASIAN BUSINESS SERIES

Doing Business with the Chinese:
A Taiwan Handbook for Executives
(Second Edition, 1990)

Doing Business with the Koreans:
A Handbook for Executives
(Second Edition, 1991)

Doing Business in Singapore:
A Handbook for Executives
(1990)

Doing Business with the Thais:
A Handbook for Executives
(1992)

Patton Pacific Press, Inc.
6766 Green Wood Lane
Sebastopol, California 95472
(707) 887-0677

Printed in the United States of America

ISBN 0-9614074-5-X
Library of Congress Catalog Card Number 91-67321
First Printing

TABLE OF CONTENTS

INTRODUCTION

This book is written for American business people who plan to do business with Thais. It is designed to help those who have not previously dealt with Thais overcome anxiety and engage in cross-cultural business more effectively.

In recent years the Thai economy has exploded with double-digit growth. Per capita gross domestic product, about $1600 in 1992, though high for Asia, is still growing. Some five thousand new factories per year open in Thailand. Bangkok, its capital and major port, is clogged with goods. Swarming with foreign business people, it has the feel of a frontier boom town.

Things were not always so. When I first visited Thailand in 1958, its economy was as backwater as its klongs. But soon Japan's economy erupted, washing a tsunami of modernization across the coasts of Asia. In its wake, such nations as Korea, Taiwan, Singapore, and Thailand awoke from long slumber to a new world. Animated by incredible new technologies, invigorated by modern entrepreneurs, and energized by the spirit of private enterprise, these nations now challenge such business behemoths as Japan, the United States, and the European Economic Community.

The first part of this book describes cultural and social factors which affect doing business in Thailand. Who can doubt that culture plays a profound role in shaping a nation's economy? Nations with prodigious natural resources such as Mexico, Russia, and Brazil often verge on economic collapse. Yet others, with few natural resources, such as Japan, Taiwan, and Singapore, produce successful, dynamic economies. If the people of Hong Kong were given Mexico, Mexico would soon have a world-class economy. Such is the power of culture.

Culture, a product of history, is passed from generation to generation by such institutions as the family, schools, and religion. The business behavior of your Thai counterpart will be profoundly conditioned by the culture he or she learned as a child. To do business with Thais you need to learn how Thai culture affects Thai behavior.

The second part of this book deals with the economic and business environment in Thailand. It explains how the Thai economy and business system originated and developed, successes, problems, opportunities, and pitfalls. Of particular importance are Thailand's business procedures, bargaining techniques, and sources of help. These, too, are rooted in culture.

The third and final section is concerned with your personal experience of Thailand: travel tips; things to do, see, and learn; living conditions, useful addresses, and recommended reading. This section should help you adjust to Thailand, particularly if you were not too excited about going there in the first place!

This book is based primarily on interviews with American and Thai business people and government officials. It is designed to get you started and to serve as a general guide. Since no two situations are exactly the same, this book does not provide solutions to specific business problems. It intends to provide helpful facts and ideas not legal advice. Conditions in Thailand are constantly changing. There are new government regulations almost daily. Organizations listed should be contacted for the most recent information.

This book does not represent the views of any agencies of the governments of Thailand or the United States. Money is denominated in U.S. dollars unless otherwise indicated.

Part One

Knowing Your Thai Counterpart

Thai business people have different goals and procedures from ours because their culture espouses different values. Before you begin your business dealings with Thais, you will want to learn everything you can about them. How do these people view themselves, their families, society, work, culture, and politics? Thai attitudes toward these institutions have a profound impact on the way they do business.

All people are socially conditioned as children. This cultural imprinting, though mostly subconscious, has a powerful effect on human behavior. When people from different cultures do business, each behaves according to cultural patterns learned in childhood. If you understand your counterpart's cultural conditioning you will have a decided advantage.

Many books on cross-cultural business stress lists of "dos and don'ts." While helpful, such lists have limited value due to the wide variety of business situations one may encounter. This book attempts to provide some depth of understanding. Learning about another culture is never easy. Cultures are vast, deep, and complicated. But once you have learned about the Thais, you will obtain much more than a business advantage. You will receive, as a bonus, a new understanding of your own culture. Your perspective on life will never be the same.

1. *Knowing Your Counterpart:* Culture and Society

The Land

When the winds are easterly the landing approach to Bangkok's Don Muang Airport descends athwart the Chao Phya River. Jets whistling, one's plane passes over tiny boats towing barges precariously loaded with rice, sagging gunwales awash with warm water. The edge of the airport is fringed with gilded tassel: needle-thin spires and gabled roofs of ancient Buddhist temples. This timeworn border contains the hubs and spokes of a modern air terminal. Green fairways, braided between gray runways, are speckled with myriads of miniature golfers, clubs furiously swinging. The scene is much like Thai life, a strange weave of old and new: Western sports and Asian arts, steel skyscrapers amid marble temples, hamburgers with lemon grass. It is an unfinished mosaic in which diverse pieces—spiritual and sensual, traditional and modern, toil and play—vie for key places in the pattern.

Thailand (Siam) is not a small nation. The third largest nation in Southeast Asia, it is the size of Spain. Its population, about fifty-nine million, also like Spain's, is third largest in the region. Thailand extends more than a thousand miles from Burma and Laos in the north to Malaya in the south; it stretches more than five hundred miles east to west. Mountain ranges, formed in the frigid Tibetan northern highlands, flay south until peaks powdered with sugary snow are replaced with green crags draped in verdure. In the center lies a low plain, the rice bowl of Asia. A long peninsula in the south is tightly bound by cobalt seas. Ironically, Thailand is shaped like its royal symbol, the elephant; its ears reach to Laos and its trunk falls to Malaya.

Thailand has a tropical climate with three seasons. During the wet monsoon period, from June to November, storms billow in from seas to the south and west, blowing walls of water, black sheets of ink into flooded fields. Paddies soon burst, green with rice. In late November the monsoon winds abruptly reverse, bringing cool, dry air from the northern mountains. The showers cease. Slowly spring arrives. By April it is hot. The land is parched, as if in a kiln. All living things wither and wait, aching for water to be released by June rains. It is no wonder that the Thai possess a religion of endless cycles, revolving wheels, and interminable reincarnations. For here all the rhythms of life follow the heartbeat of the monsoon.

Village Life

Thailand is still a nation of villages. So I visited one. The night seemed cushioned in velvet, dark and silent, tropically humid, awash with sleep. I soon slumbered in a cocoon of white gauze, mosquitoes at bay. Hours later a child shrieked in the night, obsessed with the sound of its high-pitched voice. A puppy accepted the challenge with a shrill whine. The strident duet wailed high above the leafy hamlet, prodding distant clouds to respond with deep, percussive claps of thunder. Soon the child, the dog, and the peal from the sky were joined by the sharp metallic staccato of rain on tin roofs. Dawn broke. The village awoke.

First light turned the murk to forms. Houses on raised platforms provided ground-level pens for animals and protection from snakes and floods. The yards had areas dedicated to distinct activities such as vegetable gardening, rice threshing, burning of waste, food storage, and livestock. A nearby creek flowed through groves of coconuts, mangos, and bananas. Fruit, ripe and heavy, hung from the trees. My host told me that some villagers owned more of this prosperity than others. Yet no one owned most of the land while neighbors owned none.

Women soon cooked rice in clay ovens. The first pots were offered to saffron-clad monks, morning mendicants. Second pots steamed as children started chores feeding chickens and ducks. The men prepared tools for the day's work. Men and children ate as women bathed in the stream. Some went to the fields while others went to fish or market. Children left for school. An old person in each family stayed home to watch the children, mill rice, tend fire, wash clothes, and till vegetables.

Noon was hot and dry. The sun, a melting red ball, flushed and fiery, dominated the hamlet, bathing it in a bright liquid light. There was no lunch. People napped to avoid the heat. If it had been the season for planting, plowing, and harvesting, the workers would have been in the fields and lunch would have been brought to them.

By late afternoon the villagers were home. Evening meals of rice, curry, vegetables, bits of duck were finished before dark. The setting sun, filtering through dusty air, lent a lilac tint, the color of old movies. Cool evening mists, collecting over the creek, coiled between the bamboo brakes, where night already reigned. In the murk of the banana groves bent bonzes lighted brush-wood fires. Flickering flames reflected on their golden robes. Outside the smoke squadrons of mosquitoes sortied under the attap palms.

This season the villagers had little to do but talk with and about each other. When night fell my host lighted a kerosene lamp. Neighbors arrived to visit, talk, and share rice wine and betel nut. To avoid becoming a topic of conversation everyone showed up. Much time was devoted to jokes, dirty or the slip-on-the-banana-peel type. But lewdness was not valued for its own sake. Even the best Thai literature has no counterpart to Rabelais.

Slowly the lamps went out. Except for a barking dog the village was silent. In the darkness my host reminded everyone of the cock fight on Sunday.

Half of all Thai still farm such villages. Their rice is still a major export. When they work in the cities they demand the same communal life based on instinct and tradition with no plan.

Thai Origins

In ancient times the ancestors of the Thai established the Kingdom of Nan Chao, "South of the Clouds," in southern China. In the thirteenth century Kublai Khan's Mongols pressured the Thai to move south, where they pacified Khmer and Mon aborigines and founded the Kingdom of Lan Na, "the Million Rice Fields." Here in what is now northern Thailand the Thai developed societies in order to fill the need to coordinate rice production.

Early Thai pioneers settled the new land in much the same way Americans settled their West, in small groups, creating communities like the one just described, along the way. Both frontiers produced individuals who were independent, self-reliant, and resistant to outside political pressure, pragmatic people more concerned with cultivating crops than cultivating theories about what they were doing. Women, like elephants, achieved considerable status because they were scarce and because they shared the work. Unless the Thai pioneer wanted to be his own beast of burden, he had to obtain an elephant or a wife.

The Thai brought a culture with them. But they were easily influenced by two giant neighbors, India and China. Theravada Buddhism and the concept of absolute monarchy were derived from Indian based cultures in nearby Burma and Cambodia. The Thai language is related to Chinese. The Thai continued to draw on Sinic culture from nearby Vietnam and southern China; the Thai family system is influenced by Chinese ideas. Thai royal and upper class families still carry Chinese blood.

Festivals and Holidays

Some years ago Thailand changed its calendar to correspond with the West's. The New Year is now celebrated on the first day of January. On New Year's Eve houses are cleaned and the refuse of the old year is burned. Early morning on the first day people bring food to the monks at the temples. Statues of Buddha are sprinkled with water. Young Thais honor the old by pouring perfumed water on their palms.

The Chinese New Year, based on the lunar calendar, falls in February or March. *Mahka Bucha,* in February, commemorates the start of the season for pilgrimages to Buddha's Footprint Shrine. It marks the day the Buddha first preached his doctrines.

April produces two holidays, Chakri Day, on the sixth, celebrates the founding of the reigning Chakri Dynasty. The Festival of Songkran, on the thirteenth, is the water-throwing time. It often gets out of control. People are drenched with copious volumes. Foreigners are greatly honored by being soaked to the skin. So keep your camera in a plastic bag.

May has three holidays: Labor Day, on the first; the Coronation Festival (honoring the coronation of His Majesty King Bhumibol in 1950) on the fifth; and the Rice Festival on the twelfth. In the full moon of May or early June Thais celebrate Visakha Puja Day, which honors the birth, enlightenment, and death of Buddha. At night the temples are brightened by the gleam of candlelight processions.

The First Plowing Ceremony is held at the start of the rainy season, usually late May or early June. In an elaborate ceremony the Lord of Plowing breaks the first soil of the season, scatters rice in the furrows, and begs the gods for abundant rain.

The Mid Year Celebration occurs on the first of July. The month of July also features *Khao Phansa (Asalha Puja)* which marks the start of the three-month Buddhist holy season, a type of Lent. Mother's Day is held with the Queen's Birthday on the twelfth of August.

In October or November, at the end of Buddhist Lent, the *Kathin* ceremonies are held. The monks, who have spent three months meditating in monasteries, are presented with new robes and permitted to travel. In the royal *Kathin* ceremony the king, in a barge garnished in gold, delivers gorgeous new robes to the monks of the royal temples.

The Festival of Chulalongkorn falls on the twenty-third of October. This holiday honors a monarch who introduced many reforms such as the abolition of slavery.

On the first full moon of November *Loy Krathong* is celebrated. This festival, of animistic origins, represents an attempt to propitiate the spirits of the waters in order to avoid floods. For this is the climax of the rainy season and the soils are saturated; rivers and klongs are clogged. *Krathong,* boats of banana leaves, are floated in waterways. Often they contain lighted candles, flowers, or incense sticks creating a carnival atmosphere.

In December there are three holidays: the King's birthday (also Father's Day) on the fifth; Constitution Day (recalling Thailand's first constitution in 1932) on the tenth; and New Year's Eve on the thirty-first.

The hill people of northern Thailand have their own festivals. There are many other regional celebrations: Chiang Mai's Flower Festival in early February; the Ayutthaya and Pattaya Festivals in April; the Phichit Boat Races and Phuket Vegetarian Festival in September; and the gargantuan elephant round up in Surin, in the northeast in November.

For Thais these festivals link the past to the present and give meaning to the future. But they are more than milestones for a culture. They represent an excuse for community gatherings, family reunions, and courtship for the young. If you manage Thai employees they will ask for considerable time off for these celebrations.

Religions

About ninety-five per cent of the people of Thailand are Buddhist. There are more Buddhists in Thailand than any other nation. Thailand is the only country in the world where the king is required by the constitution to be a Buddhist.

There are a quarter of a million monks in twenty thousand temples. All young Thai men are encouraged to become monks for part of their lives. Most become "rainy season" monks who enter monasteries for a few months.

Businesses in Thailand usually allow young male employees three or four months off for this purpose. This is done on a one-time basis.

Buddhists are convinced that ultimate realities cannot be expressed in words. They think verbalized doctrines tend to obscure, rather than reveal, sublime truths. By not requiring unlimited belief in narrow dogmas, Buddhism became a broad religion of unlimited tolerance which appealed to people of many cultures. In not seeking to dominate the daily lives of its adherents, as contemporary Islam and Christianity sought to do, Buddhism succeeded in merging with and transforming such disparate beliefs as Chinese Taoism, Japanese Shinto, and the god-king cults of Southeast Asia.

Buddhism is an ancient belief; 1992 was its 2535th year. Gautama Buddha did not consider himself to be a god and he did not ask people to worship him. Buddhism, which has no god, began as a protest against Hinduism, which has many. Buddha rebelled against the rigid Hindu caste system and dogma of predestination. In time Buddhism split into two branches: Mahayana (big wheel) and Hinayana (little wheel). Hinayana, also called Theraveda Buddhism, which is now practiced in Thailand, eventually lost its social message, stopped opposing earthly inequities, and became a religion of withdrawal, contemplation, and meditation. For it, salvation became an individual endeavor.

Buddhism defines human existence as suffering. To help the individual seek a better destiny Buddha expounded The Law, symbolized by a revolving wheel of life. It spins in ceaseless cycles of human fate, creating blurs of death and reincarnation which absorb individuals into universes of heavens and hells, then reshapes them into new humans or animals with no memories of previous existences.

In a way the wheel of life is a rack of one's own creation, the result of individual desire. The most burning wish of all, to break free of the wheel, represents a Catch-22 situation; the more one lusts for release, the tighter one is bound to the wheel. The wheel of life never stops. One spins and suffers, twists and turns, tormented through endless incarnations. Finally, some dedicated souls succeed in extinguishing every iota of desire and individuality. Only then, one who is no longer one, finds freedom, flying off into nothingness, extinction, a black hole called nirvana; for Buddhists, a consummation devoutly to be wished.

In Western religions, such as Christianity, people seek salvation by transcending nature and saving the soul. In Eastern religions, such as Buddhism, people find spiritual peace by accepting nature and extinguishing the soul.

Most Thai Buddhists find oblivion too much to hope for. They see no chance to escape the wheel. So they concentrate on gaining merit to help them achieve a better *karma* (or fate) for the next reincarnation. Failing this, some Buddhists will try to create merit to increase the joys and reduce the sorrows of this life; many actually prefer this alternative.

The system of gaining religious merit operates almost on a point system. Feeding monks is not considered charity, for one gains merit. Merit is also earned by going to temple, serving in the priesthood, gluing gold leaf to statues of Buddha, contributing money for new temples, and releasing caged birds (for a fee).

About a quarter of all rural income goes to earning merit. Funds derived in this way benefit Buddhist wats, which not only contain temples, but quarters for monks, cooking facilities, schools, social centers, charity facilities for the poor, and crematoria. Many of the functions of wats are not directly religious. Some even involve community entertainment.

In crisis or sickness many Thai will not rely on their stores of merit. In deep-seated superstition they rely on ancient animistic beliefs. Indeed, Thai Buddhism and Hinduism incorporate them. The First Plowing Ceremony and *Loy Krathong* are based on magical concepts.

Hinduism and Buddhism were originally imported to Thailand from India partly because of their mystical cosmologies. These religions succeeded by absorbing and syncretizing indigenous Thai animistic beliefs. Thai Buddhism is so tolerant that the nation's monarchs have often given donations to other religions, and Christian missionaries have been allowed to preach in Buddhist temples. Since ancient times Thailand has been a crossroad for many cultures. Such great variety has given the nation the ability to tolerate, absorb, and modify any single influence.

About five per cent of all Thai are Muslims. These people are concentrated in the south, along the long peninsula Thailand shares with Malaya. Islam was most successful in insular and coastal areas of Southeast Asia because it was brought by Muslim sea traders who refused to deal with infidels. Islam never penetrated the interior of Thailand, where Hindu and Buddhist beliefs survived with great vitality.

Islam was founded by the Prophet Muhammad in the seventh century. The Koran, the holy book of Islam, prescribes a religion which enters every aspect of the lives of its faithful through a strict code called *sharia*. In the Middle East *sharia* is practiced with a compulsive passion. But the Thais have modified it and practice a softer form. Muslim Thai women do not wear veils. Dietary restrictions are less severe. Even the primary pillar of the Islamic belief, its stringent belief in Allah, the One God, is not fully upheld. Muslim village leaders in southern Thailand will often open a feast by invoking the divine blessings of various and sundry kitchen gods, house spirits, tree gnomes, water nymphs, and ancestor ghosts. Only after this motley array of deities has been propitiated will the prayer end piously, with the basic Islamic credo: "There is no God but Allah and Muhammad is his prophet!"

In general the Thai feeling about religion is enjoyable, casual, and relaxed, stressing village festivals and community meetings at wats and mosques. But Thai religion can create sensitive situations which will require you to take thought and care. Do not give a Thai employee a hearty and encouraging slap on the back. Do not pat his or her cute little child on the head. The spirits thus disturbed would bedevil your business forever. Never point the soles of your feet or toes at anyone. They are not considered clean because they may have crushed and killed insects. So keep your feet flat on the floor or sit with both legs to one side. Women should never touch a monk. When giving objects to monks they should set them down within reach.

It is strange that Buddhism, an ancient religion, thrives so well in modern Thailand. It has made an adroit transition from rice field to factory. Buddha images, decked with flower offerings and incense, are ubiquitous. Employees pray at company spirit houses, carry photos of favorite monks, and make pilgrimages to favorite temples, a unifying force for a business.

Language

Many languages other than Thai are spoken in Thailand. As the agricultural Thai settled the lowlands and river valleys, the earlier, more primitive hunter-gatherers kept to the highlands. Each spoke its own language. Even today the distribution pattern of languages follows elevation contours like a geodetic survey. The map includes languages of the Tachins, Karens, and Lolos; Miaos and Yaos; remnants of the Chams, who speak a language related to Polynesian; and Malayan in the south.

But Thai language dominates the heartland, is taught in the schools, and provides social cohesion. It is a poetic language, replete with similes, metaphors, parables, and puns. Its most popular genre is *like,* the common poetry of the market place. Folk sayings include "don't give diamonds to monkeys" and "black dogs are ill omens." A favorite saying is *mai pen rai,* "it does not matter."

The Thai language uses tones to indicate meaning in the same way as Chinese with which it is related. The same words will have different meanings depending upon the tones used for each syllable. There are five tones in Thai: high (/), falling (^), middle (no mark), rising (v), and low (\). A word may have one or more syllables.

At an early time the Thais used Chinese characters. But, under the influence of Indian traders and monks, they soon dropped Chinese characters in favor of Sanskrit and Pali scripts. In written Thai the spoken tones are indicated by the diacritical marks represented above. These are written above the consonants in each syllable. The final version of modern written Thai was developed under King Ramkamheng in the thirteenth century.

Like Chinese, the grammar of modern Thai is simple. There are no inflections, such as verb conjugations, noun declensions, singular or plural; no changes in case, gender, mood, or tense. But there are numerous complicated honorific words designed to indicate social class and status. Sentences are arranged in the order of subject, verb, and object with adjectives following nouns. The same word may serve a variety of functions depending upon its position in a sentence. Thai names are rumored to be the longest in the world.

Thai has several dialects. Standard Thai is spoken in Bangkok and central Thailand. People in the north, northeast, and south speak regional dialects but standard Thai is used for government and mass communications. Many educated Thai speak English. The Chinese minority speak a variety of Chinese languages.

The Arts

Long before the Thai entered the area, there was art in what is now Thailand. As early as the sixth century, Dvaravati (Mon) people developed traditions of dance, drama, architecture, sculpture, and painting. These art forms were based upon Hindu and Buddhist myths. Several centuries later the Khmers from Cambodia invaded the area, bringing with them the unique Khmer architecture typified by Angkor Wat. Today these Khmer influences survive in the ruins of Lopburi, Sukhothai, and Pimai. In southern Thailand the art of the Srivijaya kingdom, based in Malaya and Sumatra, was dominant. In time this area fell under Islamic influence.

When the Thai people moved south from Yunnan into Thailand they brought with them both Chinese and Burmese styles of art. Most Thai kings have encouraged the arts. King Narai sponsored poetry schools. King Trailok's reign in the fifteenth century was a golden age for art.

In the past century or so there have been many Western influences. The 1932 coup led to a freer and more modern style of expression. Artists such as Kamol Tassananchalee introduced American concepts.

The late Tang Chang's paintings range from colorful outdoor scenes to abstracts executed with such speed and violence that marks made by his fingers, hands, and knees can be seen on the canvas.

Music, Dance, and Drama

Thai music, dance and drama were developed to serve the needs of royalty and religion.

A Thai orchestra consists of woodwinds such as the *pi nai* (a kind of oboe), percussion instruments such as the *ranad* (a type of xylophone), and a variety of drums, cymbals, and gongs. Such orchestras provide music for the Thai popular dance known as the *ramwong*. Couples form a circle. The female dancer glides around the circle while her male partner, in turn, dances around her. They never touch but the movement of the two concentric circles and the classical motions of heads, hands, and arms create the impression of fine lace in motion.

In classical Thai theater acting and dancing often overlap as one. In *Khon* drama the actors wear head masks while offstage players recite the script. In *Lakhon* only the non-human characters, such as monkeys, wear masks. Both forms of drama commonly use the *Ramayana* as a topic. This is a long adventure story about the Hindu god Vishnu (reincarnated as Prince Rama), the goddess-princess Sita, Hanuman (a flying monkey), and Ravana (the demon king).

Drama and film today use modern light, sound, and set designs for performances of traditional works. For the past thirty years Seree Vangnaitham has stimulated the development of Thai drama, music dance, and poetry. He has written and composed over a thousand pieces.

Literature

Thailand's literary tradition goes back to the thirteenth century. Much literature was based on Buddhist topics.

Notable examples are *Kotmai Tra Sam Duang*, a book on Buddhist ethics; *Jataka,* stories of Buddha's numerous births; and a body of poetry drawing on the story of the *Ramayana.*

Other stories, such as the *Phra Law* (royal romance), used Thai royalty as a subject. *Khun Chang, Khun Phaen* is a title which includes the names of two men in love with the same woman. Thailand's greatest poet was Sunthon Phu, who wrote the epic romance *Phra Aphai Mani* in the early nineteenth century. Development of the modern Thai novel was encouraged by King Vajiravudh in the early part of this century. Novels such as Dotmai Sot's *Phudi* (the genteel) focus on the realities of modern Thai life.

Architecture, Sculpture, and Painting

Thai architecture, sculpture, and painting also serve religion and royalty. Thai temples, with spires of gold gleaming in the sun, epitomize the best Buddhist architecture; devout structures, their soaring roofs and marble walls withstand worldly heat, keeping the sanctuaries they encase cool, dim, and placid.

Sculptures of Buddha are highly stylized; meanings follow postures. Buddhas assume one of four positions: standing, walking, reclining, and sitting. Their gestures embody a system of symbols which span two dozen centuries. A seated Buddha, with right hand over right leg, fingers down and left hand over crossed leg, palm up gives witness to enlightenment. The standing Buddha, with one hand raised, palm open, fingers pointed skyward, dissolves fear; with *both* hands raised the same Buddha helps one overcome cravings. Notable examples of these include the 160 foot long Reclining Buddha at Wat Po, the Emerald

Buddha at Wat Phra Keo, and the Golden Buddha at Wat Trimitr. All are in Bangkok.

Monks paint murals on wat walls to teach Buddhism. An excellent example is the wall mural in the gallery of the Temple of the Emerald Buddha in Bangkok. Thai people support such traditional Buddhist art to gain religious merit. Since there is no reward for subsidizing pictures of Pepsi bottles, pop art receives little sustenance. Sculptures of The Buddha will not soon be replaced by avant-garde contraptions of cables.

Cultural Change

When I first visited Thailand in 1958 it was a rural nation of about twenty million people raising rice, a land of spices and springtime, of picture book pagodas and sacred white elephants. Bangkok, *Krung Thep*, City of the Angels, was a scenic town crossed with canals, the Venice of the East. Teak boats, with canvas canopies, crawled along the klongs, pausing at times to market packs of fruits and vegetables to merchants set up under the shade of the attap palms which lined the shores. Old women, viand venders in wicker hats, hawked tasty snacks to the *farang*, their term for the foreigners who came to visit the temples. It was a serene place. The Vietnam War and Thailand's economic boom lay far in the future.

Since my first visit the population of Thailand has almost tripled to about fifty-nine million. Many of the klongs in Bangkok have been filled to furnish streets for the heavy traffic. Smog and noise spew up between shoddy highrises. The city is on the make, a hustling industrial boom town, complete with slums and crime gangs. Vice is a major industry supporting thousands of drug lords and gambling dealers, and, by some accounts, as many as half a million prostitutes.

Many Thai, though nominally Buddhists, now prefer to accumulate, rather than renounce worldly goods. Many have cosmopolitan tastes. The interests of your Thai business counterpart may range from compact disks of Mozart to the latest antics of the Chicago Cubs.

So there is cultural conflict. The collective programming of the mind which we call culture defines human societies. It is passed, as patterns of thought and behavior, from parents to children, and is crystallized in social institutions such as the family, the school, the temple, and the work place. The process of acculturation is powerful, pervasive, and insidious because it often passes subconsciously between generations.

But culture also changes. It is shaped by a *dynamic* relationship between the past and present, indigenous and foreign, individuals and institutions. Once change begins a ricochet effect magnifies the transformation; morals, mores, and manners are modified. Sacred beliefs, stretched to answer new situations, snap and break. For a while the world seems to go awry. Then a new culture, a reincarnation of the old, emerges, and a society finds a new way of life. Such is the state of life in Thailand today.

2. *Knowing Your Thai Counterpart:* Family Life

Family Structure

The Thai family is less extended than the Chinese family. Though the family may involve three generations while the grandparents are alive, most couples prefer their own homes. The Thai kinship system is quite loose. Family loyalty, though genuine, is not as strong as most Asian family systems. People who are only distantly related or not related at all often live together as a family. Members of rural families may move to the cities but will keep contact with their villages.

Thais, like Americans, are little concerned about lineage and ancestry. Thai family names are no part of tradition; they were introduced by royal decree in 1916.

Thai families share sexual equality more than others in Asia. The women are often the strong ones in the family.

They participate in both field work and housework. Many Thai men have reputations for laziness.

The man may be the head of the house in name, but the woman usually handles the finances. Women have equal rights regarding land ownership, divorce, and inheritance. Respect is rendered, not by sex, but on the basis of earned religious merit and age. Family decisions are usually derived from extensive discussion of all adult members. The relative equality of Thai women is in part due to the shortage of females when the first settlers, mainly men, came down from China.

The Thai Home

The Thai home was originally a village hut on stilts. Today many Thai live in apartments, town houses, and condominiums. Yet old traditions endure. When visiting a Thai home remove your shoes before entering. Be sure to step over, not on, the threshold, because that is where the home spirit lives. It is usually not necessary to bring a gift though flowers or sweets for children are appreciated. Do not praise your host's possessions, or she or he will feel obligated to give them to you as a gift.

Only more Westernized Thais shake hands. The traditional Thai greeting is the *wai*, consisting of clasped hands, prayer-like, pressed to the chest or lower face, and a slight bow. The higher the hands, the lower the head, the more respect. But tips of the fingers must never be above eye level. A *wai* must always be returned. It can be used for greeting, apology, thanks, or goodby.

When in a Thai home one must be careful about manners. Do not cross your legs or point a foot or sole at others. Do not use your feet to move things or to touch people. Do not touch a Thai's head or pass anything over it; it is considered the sacred abode of the *khwan*, or body spirit.

At a Thai meal the spoon is held in the right hand. The fork, in the left, is used to push food on the spoon. Since food is served in small pieces knives are not needed. In northern Thailand people eat rice with their fingers. Chinese Thai use chopsticks. Always leave a small amount of food on your plate to show you have had enough.

Birth and Early Childhood

For Buddha life was to be a gradual process with few rites of passage. He provided no ceremonies for birth, death, or marriage. So Buddhist monks often participate in *Hindu* ceremonies. These are held at homes rather than wats.

At birth the baby is washed, wrapped in swaddling clothes, and set in a bamboo basket. A three-day-long naming ritual takes place several months after the birth.

Children under three are treated permissively, encouraged by example, not forced. Though they are taught to be polite and respect their elders, they are raised with more independence and self-reliance than in the traditional Chinese system. Serious socialization begins at three or four with mild punishments for deliberate acts of disobedience. Children learn to show respect for parents, monks, and elders by rendering a *wai* with hands clasped at the correct height on chest or face. By age four children usually play in groups of the same age. There is little sibling rivalry. Siblings and cousins are very close. By age seven or eight boys help in the field and girls assist with house chores. At this age most enter primary school.

Education

The government requires all children to attend one to three years of kindergarten and six years of primary school. Until the 1920s primary education was run by the wats and involved memorization of Buddhist scriptures. Today education is primarily a governmental responsibility.

The system follows the 6-3-3 pattern. Six years of primary school followed by an optional three years of junior high and three years of senior high. Secondary schools require considerable tuitions so some Thai cannot attend. Nevertheless, the literacy rate is high.

In recent years the government has shifted some education from traditional academics to technical training. There are now many vocational schools for skills development in such fields as machine tools, construction, graphic arts, and electronics. These programs include apprenticeships for on-the-job training.

Competition for college is by examination and is very rigorous. Chulalongkorn University is considered the best college. MBA programs are offered by Thammasatad Chulalongkorn University. The Asian Institute of Technology (AITC) functions as a center for advanced technical training for the ASEAN organization, consisting of Indonesia, Malaysia, the Philippines, Singapore, and Thailand.

Adolescence

Thai children graduate from primary schools as young teenagers. Unlike Americans, who dress and behave to show individual self-expression, young Thai are raised to be polite and subdued. They dress to fit into a smoothly conforming society. Thai dress and demeanor are softer and subtler than ours. It is best to adjust to these patterns when in Thai society.

Because Buddhism teaches that craving brings suffering, many Thai parents do not pressure their children to achieve. They learn to avoid competition because it may involve loss of face for the loser. American managers say they find it difficult to develop a spirit of competition among Thai employees.

At eighteen all males register for the military draft. Those who are selected will see some of the nation outside their villages or neighborhoods. For many boys adolescence ends with ordination into the *Sangha,* the Buddhist monkhood. Tradition encourages all young men to enter at some time in their lives. Most enter monasteries for only a few months. One need only be a minimum of twenty years of age, healthy, solvent, and have parental permission. Becoming a priest, even temporarily, represents admission to adulthood. Like the military, the *Sangha* provides social and geographic mobility for young men.

Young women enter adulthood through a process of increasing independence and involvement in family responsibilities. Many now enter college and the business world.

Recreation

Thai people have a zest for life, a lively sense of humor. They are fun loving people who enjoy gambling, theater, travel, and sports. They avidly participate in lotteries, card games, coin tossing, and animal fights. They fight crickets and fish as well as cocks.

The most popular sports are volleyball, soccer, Ping-Pong, and badminton. They also enjoy kite fighting, martial arts (such as Thai boxing), and *takro*, which involves keeping a wicker ball in the air without use of one's hands.

Thais love to travel. They consider themselves part of a larger society, not always tied to one community. One advantage of being a monk is the chance to wander and receive gifts of food.

Courtship and Marriage

Much courtship takes place at the frequent festivals and feasts. At these times families from outlying areas swarm into villages and cities. Young people have an opportunity to socialize. Once couples pair off the early courtship may take place under the eyes of the girl's parents. Western-style dating has recently become popular in the larger cities. Thailand is the only developing nation of Asia which allows access to contraceptives by youth of all ages, married or not.

There are many marriage patterns. Usually the prospective groom must obtain approval of the prospective bride's family. Go-betweens are sometimes used. Elopement and living together without marriage are not unusual and are generally accepted. Most Thais are married by their early twenties.

The time and date of the marriage are often arranged by an astrologer. The bride's family pays for the wedding. The groom's family provides an endowment for the couple. A Buddhist monk may consecrate the couple before the wedding. But the ceremony is vaguely Hindu.The couple usually kneels over a bronze or silver bowl, hands held together. A white cord is wound about both their heads bringing their spirits together. Each guest pours a little lustral water over the clasped hands of the couple. After a sumptuous banquet the guests are given small gifts. The marriage may or may not be registered. Couples may live together and start a family without benefit of a ceremony.

Old Age and Death

Old age usually begins at sixty. Then designation as head of the household will pass to a younger family member. The grandparents will work a bit around the house but will spend more and more time at the temple, hands veined and dry as fallen leaves, clasped in prayer. Thai in old age seek a final consecration of life and acceptance of death. In order to ensure a good reincarnation dying people try to direct their final thoughts to the Buddha and his teachings.

As in the West, a death brings social unity. Distant family members return home. The work of the entire village or neighborhood is needed to discharge obligations and perform proper rites. Cremation ceremonies are expensive; the cost must be borne by the extended family. Since there are no Buddhist death rites, Buddhist monks will participate (at the fringes) of traditional Hindu ceremonies.

The body is bathed and dressed in white. Saffron-robed monks intone ancient chants. The wake, a vigil with visitors, lasts all night. The next day the corpse is placed on an ornately decorated bier and burned to ashes. A few days later a ceremony and feast are held at the house of the deceased.

What Kind of Person?

What kind of person does the Thai family produce? Its product is very different from ours. Thais lack Western-style egos. But, like us, they are self-reliant, looking to themselves first to solve problems. Like us, they are individuals. But they express themselves in different ways.

An American will assert his individuality with a blatant belligerence. Thais do it through aloof detachment, *Chai Yen,* a "cool heart." They exude a quiet dignity, a soft politeness, a gentle grace. If you manage Thai people you must be sensitive or you will misunderstand many situations.

Some Thai characteristics seem contradictory. Thais readily accept hierarchies and show instant and deep respect for authority. One would think that they would easily accept regimentation and the "time is money" constraints of modern business. But they do not. *Any* discipline is hard to accept because Thais find pleasure only when life is spontaneous. Behind your back they will call your agenda, itineraries, and schedules "mother's lists." Yet they will rebel passively, by subtle noncompliance. As soon as a new work project stops being fun, the Thai worker may lose enthusiasm and drift away.

The flexible Thai seem to have two distinct patterns of behavior, one for peers and one for people deserving great respect. Thai behavior with peers is probably closer and more relaxed than similar American relationships. But, when confronted with a social superior, the Thai personality quickly changes, showing an extreme deference bordering on obsequiousness.

Thai people are much concerned about gaining religious merit and following the path of Buddha. Yet, like advocates of other religions, they can be very selective about which spiritual practices and prohibitions they choose to obey. Some are part-time Buddhists.

In general Thai people are serene and peaceful, humble and considerate, taking care not to hurt. Within this pattern of behavior they sometimes operate so indirectly that some Westerners consider them to be devious and deceptive. Together these people constitute a society that flows; that, with some exceptions, is freely formed and loosely structured; that requires a minimum of obligations. Thai life is spontaneous, not controlled; enjoyed, not endured; lived for the present, not the past or future.

3. *Knowing Your Thai Counterpart:* **Politics and Law**

What's in a Name? Thailand and Siam

When the first Thai people moved into Southeast Asia, the Khmer people were already there. A Khmer inscription on a twelfth century temple at Angkor Wat refers to the Thai as *syam*, meaning dark brown people. In A.D. 1283 the Thai overthrew Khmer rule and founded the Kingdom of Sukhothai. Here they first called themselves "Thai," meaning "free," to differentiate themselves from their compatriots to the east who were still under Khmer rule.

Until 1939 the official name of the country was Siam. Then it was changed to Thailand. This may have been motivated by a program to expand the nation's borders in order to free ethnic Thai living in nearby nations. In 1946 the government changed the name back to Siam; in 1949, back to Thailand. But sometimes Siam is still used.

Early Political History

The Thai political system began largely in response to the need to build and administer the intricate systems of irrigation canals required to produce wet-rice. This required detailed coordination of community labor. Siamese royalty was so successful in performing this duty that Thailand usually had huge rice surpluses available for export.

In 1350 the capital was moved south from Sukhothai to Ayutthaya in order to escape an epidemic. A golden age followed which lasted until 1767 when invading Burmese burned Ayutthaya to the ground. The Thai heritage, history, art, and literature disappeared in the conflagration and the nation disintegrated into petty states. Only a Chinese invasion of Burma and the emergence of a great Thai general, Phraya Taksin, prevented more disaster. Within ten years Taksin had united the Thai, moved the capital to Thon Buri, across the river from Bangkok, and seized the throne. He declared himself to be both god and king and decreed his own immortality. This megalomania was too much, even for his own ministers. They murdered Taksin. Another general, Chakki, took the throne and moved the capital to Bangkok, "the village of the wild plum." The purpose of moving the capital east of the Chao Phya River was to use the river as a moat to protect the capital from the Burmese, who always invaded from the west.

King Mongkut, who ruled from 1851 to 1868, assumed the throne after nearly thirty years as a monk. Yet he saw the need to involve Siam in the outside world. King Mongkut was extremely intelligent and an accomplished scholar in languages, science, and history. The book *Anna and the King of Siam* and the musical *The King and I* offer gross distortions because they depict King Mongkut as an ignorant barbarian who was modernized and mesmerized by a Victorian schoolmarm.

Period of Western Influence

Western influence in Thailand began in the sixteenth century with the arrival of the Portuguese, who were followed by the Spanish, Dutch, French, and English. A brief Thai relationship with European powers in the seventeenth century broke down but was followed in the nineteenth century by an active diplomatic policy which resulted in a series of treaties. The first Thai-American treaty was signed in 1833. These treaties gave Western powers special rights, such as exemptions from Thai law. There was considerable intermarriage; today many Thai families have some Western blood.

During centuries of Western imperialism, Thailand survived by becoming a neutral buffer state between Britain and France, playing off the British in Malaya and Burma against the French in Indochina. Although Thailand lost some provinces in the process, it was able to keep the core of the country independent. In all Asia, only Japan and Thailand were able to keep a reasonable degree of independence. After World War I Thailand used its role as an ally of Britain, France, and the United States to negotiate new treaties on the basis of equality.

During World War II Thailand again played two countries, Japan and the United States, off against each other. After brief resistance to the Japanese, the Thai made an accommodation with Japan.

Thailand then declared war on the United States. Since the Thai ambassador in the United States refused to transmit the Thai declaration of war to the American government, the United States never declared war on Thailand. Again Thailand had it both ways. While some of its leaders were allied with the Japanese, others supported an American-sponsored underground in Thailand.

Thailand responded to the communist takeover of China in 1949 by supporting the West. It sent troops to the United Nations army in the Korean War, joined the Southeast Asia Treaty Organization, and sent an army division to fight on the American side in the Vietnam War. Thailand also provided major air bases and recreational facilities for American forces during the Vietnam War.

After Vietnam fell Thailand expertly avoided becoming a "falling domino." It successfully stifled communist rebellions along its borders with Laos and Malaya. Using a subtle policy it kept Vietnam, Cambodia, China, and Laos so busy competing for power in Southeast Asia, none could seriously consider the conquest of Thailand.

Through its history Thailand has handled foreign pressure like a supple bamboo, bending under stress, but never breaking, saving strength and stealing time, so it could spring back into its rightful place at the first opportune moment.

The Institution of the Kingship

The institution of the kingship is closely related to Buddhism. Early Thai kings held absolute power based on their claims to be bodhisattvas, enlightened people who gave up nirvana to help others. Such monarchs could have things their own way. The Palace Law of 1450 codified rules for the royal household. Some penalties were severe: for rocking the king's boat, death; for whispering at a royal reception, death; for allowing stray dogs into the palace, death! Even today Thais who do not show respect for royalty are jailed; foreigners who lack proper reverence are visited by the police. So be careful! An incident involving the king would not be good for your business!

Thai kings were polygamous. All male children of the queen or any concubine could claim the throne. This practice caused frequent disputes.

Although the absolute monarchy ended with the revolution of 1932, most Thais remain fanatical royalists. The monarch is much loved by his people. King Bhumibol, though born in the United States and raised in Switzerland, is devoted to his people.

White Elephants

Kings and white elephants share a Thai mystique. Only a king can own one. These albinos are held in high regard because they are believed to be reincarnations of a future Buddha.

Aside from this, white elephants are worthless. Only royalty has the affluence to support them in the manner to which they are accustomed. Their egos must be pampered with expensive ceremonies. Costly cosmetics must be applied to smooth wrinkled skin. A special mascara, especially formulated for white pachyderms, beautifies their eyelashes. In ancient times a Thai king who wanted to financially ruin a competing king gave him a white elephant.

White elephants are only part of the royal regalia. Royal processions display finely tempered swords, jewelled crowns, and silk umbrellas. Gilded boats with wind-swollen sails ply the Chao Phya, spuming fountains of foam. The Thai love royal opulence. As long as the king rules, many Thai could care less about which general or politician governs.

Coups and Constitutions

In Thai tradition the system of capital punishment was sufficiently civilized to avoid a bloody mess. Condemned royalty and nobility were neatly inserted in velvet bags before being beaten to death with sandalwood clubs. Common criminals were placed in huge hollow bamboo balls which were given to the elephants for play.

Thailand's coups are like that, violence with little gore. In the famous coup of 1957 there was only one casualty, a soldier who shot himself while cleaning his rifle!

As early as the 1947 coup the procedure had been perfected and recognized as a fine art. Coup leaders no longer euphemistically called themselves "the People's Party." Instead they declared themselves "the Coup Group." In this one the prime minister survived by swimming away from a Thai navy ship under attack by the Thai air force!

The biggest coup occurred in 1932 when the government of King Prajadhipok was seized by revolutionaries during his absence from the capital. The coup leaders were young officials who had been educated in Europe, where they had observed democratic systems. They wanted a limited democracy for Thailand. They held some princes hostage until the king agreed to a constitution. The coup leaders, who called themselves "the promoters," produced a constitution which provided for a National Assembly in which half the members would be appointed by the party in power (through the king), and half the members would be elected. As literacy increased so would the percentage of elected members. This constitution recognized the importance of education and also served to keep the coup leaders in power.

Thailand now had a government which was democratic in form by not in essence. Most power remained with the military. In 1957, the public, upset by military rule, elected a democratic administration. But such democracy was "too unstable" for the military. Field Marshal Sarit led another coup and remained dictator until his death in 1963. Then General Thanom became dictator. He was overthrown in the uprising of 1973, brought about by inflation and corruption. The king supported this revolt by giving sanctuary in his palace to student leaders. The result was a constitutional government led by an elderly scholar.

For a few years there were no coups. In 1988 Premier Chatichai won election. His government lasted only two years. On February 23, 1991, the military charged Chatichai with corruption. A coup led by General Sunthorn Kongsompong removed Chatichai from office. Power passed to a National Peacekeeping Council which was dominated by the military but supportive of business. A government headed by Anand Panyarachun drew up a new constitution and set another election.

Recent Politics

On December 7, 1991, Thailand adopted a new constitution which concentrates power in a Senate appointed by the National Peacekeeping Council (the ruling junta).

Yet Thailand's political parties are now quite diverse. The Social Action Party wants to reduce rural poverty. Since there is little rural malnutrition, the other parties usually govern by coalition. Parties in the coalition, such as the National Democratic Party, the Democratic Party, and the Popular Party, divide power and patronage by ministry. Thus different departments of the Thai government will often have conflicting policies. Each government bureaucracy is vertical; there is little horizontal mesh between ministries. When your company wants approval for a business deal, one ministry may say "yes," the other, "no."

Political Prospects

Frequent coups make Thailand appear less stable than it really is. The Thai monarchy, as an institution, provides unity and continuity. King Bhumibol has been on the throne since 1946. The elite military cliques which vie for power have few ideological differences. They play a political form of musical chairs. Coups often involve such complicated plots and colorful personalities that they would make good comic operas.

Yet, changes in government seldom have much effect on common citizens. The oligarchy does not oppress the people. The use of power is softened by Buddhist precepts. The country has never had class warfare or peasant revolts. Thailand probably has more personal freedom than any other nation in the area.

Thailand is not likely to experience the kind of upheavals which recently occurred in China. The traditional Thai value of *kreng jai* encourages accommodation and compromise with both nature and mankind. The pace of political change in Thailand is likely to be slower than China's, but it will be smoother and involve less conflict. As the middle class becomes more affluent, power will follow money as it did in Taiwan and Korea.

There are two caveats to this optimistic evaluation. First, the government will have to be sure that the disparity between high urban and lower rural standards of living does not become too great. If it does not do this there could be serious political problems. Also, the government must be sure that corruption does not undermine Thailand's economic boom. While the inchoate capitalism the nation has adopted thrives on normal human greed, such activities as "squeeze," bribery, and nepotism can choke the new boom because they make market pricing, cost analysis, quality control, and information systems ineffective. Unfortunately, there is a saying in Thailand: "corruption is as common as orchids ." (This beautiful flower thrives in Thailand.)

You must not become involved in Thai politics. However, as your company's Thai specialist you will want to keep current on events and trends so you can ascertain your corporation's political opportunities and risks.

Part Two

Thailand: Business and Economy

Thailand has one of the fastest growing economies in the world. This success is due primarily to its ability to build export business. We need to learn how this is done in order to deal with our trade deficit.

In order to operate successfully in Thailand you will need an understanding of how the economy developed and how it functions, its successes and failures. This section will also help you with some of the practical problems of establishing business relationships in Thailand. These topics include information on how to get help, Thai business organization and procedures, standards of etiquette, and patterns of negotiation.

This book is designed to be a general guide and does not proffer legal advice. Every business situation is different and rules and regulations are constantly changing. More recent and more detailed information may be obtained by contacting organizations listed in the chapter on useful addresses.

As we look at the Thai business and economic environment, we must keep in mind the cultural and social perspective covered in Part I. We can only understand what is going on in the Thai business world if we approach it from the viewpoint of the Thais themselves. Here again business people are people first. Culture is again a dominant influence.

4. A Brief Economic History

Early Period

The earliest Thais were hunters and gatherers. Such people need no salt because meat has enough for humans. When they settled into agriculture, the Thais condemned themselves to one of the earliest forms of taxation, the salt levy. (People living on grain need a salt supplement.) Salt was produced primarily from the evaporation of sea water. It was therefore easy for coastal rulers to control the process and collect the tax. Such processes, which link economic needs and political power, continue today.

The ancestors of the Thai who lived in what is now southern China and northeastern Thailand were great economic innovators. Some five thousand years ago they first cultivated dry rice on the Khorat plateau. The Chinese of the same period were ignorant of rice and ate only millet. The Thai people were among the first humans to master bronze metallurgy, forging bronze (of copper and tin) in the Ban Chiang area around three thousand B.C., a thousand years before the Bronze Age began in China.

Before the Thai people entered what is now central Thailand, there were already Indian-based civilizations there which engaged in trade. An intricate trading network included Chinese merchants who sailed south along the Asian coast keeping in sight of land. Commerce was also conducted with Cambodians, Burmese, and eventually Westerners. Through it all the Thais assimilated foreign ideas and products but kept their unique identity.

The Role of Rice

Rice has always had a paramount role in the Thai economy. As the early Thais, fleeing the Mongols, moved southward through the river valleys of Southeast Asia, they turned the forests into rice fields. The need to build irrigation and levee systems for rice cultivation required a powerful king to coordinate the labor; all subjects were required to work on rice projects three months per year. Even today two out of three Thais live in the soupy heat of the central lowlands producing rice on the alluvial plain. This unique grain has always furnished the Thais with a rich food supply. In the process rice became intricately intertwined with religion, economics, and politics.

Few Westerners can fathom the special role of rice in the development of Asia. Since rice provides more calories per area than any other grain, its domestication in Neolithic times produced a "green revolution" which today nourishes teeming millions. Almost half the world depends on rice for its diet. Without it most Asians could not exist.

Intense labor is needed to plow fields, plant paddy rice, transplant and harvest. Millions of seedlings must be transplanted *one at a time*. Extensive irrigation systems must be carefully adjusted to maintain proper water levels through droughts and monsoon rains, for rice takes no nourishment from the soil; it never depletes it. Instead rice derives its sustenance from minerals and algae *in the water*. It provides nourishment to an entire continent but uses its mud only to anchor roots. This ancient relationship, more than any other, defines Asia.

Asians like it clean, pure, and as white as snow. Rice is the only grain grown exclusively for humans rather than animals. Because of it kings were coronated, religions were summoned to sanctity, and festivals were designed to commemorate its planting and harvest. The size and location of most Thai cities were dictated by economic patterns related to the cultivation and transport of rice.

Originally Thailand raised a type of rice which was so glutinous people easily ate it with their fingers. This kind of rice is still produced for local consumption in the north and northeast. But a newer, fast growing "floating rice" is now cultivated on the central plain. This rice grows so fast it is able to keep above rapidly rising monsoon flood waters. The abundant rice harvests of central Thailand allow the Thais to enjoy better living standards than their neighbors; it remains a major export.

For many Thais the great economic activity of Bangkok means less than the nation's rice production. Rice is farmed in individual plots. However, much of the work is done communally, because one family's rice needs to be transplanted or harvested before a neighbor's is ready. Villagers will work in one field, then another, keeping track of the labor time and exchanging it. Such neighborly cooperation usually involves groups of one or two dozen people. The family whose rice is being worked will provide food, drink, and entertainment to the group. Thus one Thai word, *ngan,* means both work and play. The same value, combining work and play, is carried into offices and factories by rural Thai when they migrate to the cities. Most of the Western business managers I interviewed in my 1991 trip told me this Thai attitude was their biggest problem.

Western Imperialism

The initial effects of Thailand's contact with Western powers were good. The Bowring Treaty of 1855, and similar treaties with the United States and other Western powers which followed, stimulated trade. The opening of the Suez Canal in 1869 and the development of steamships increased the market for Thailand's teak, sugar, tobacco, and tin. Toward the end of the nineteenth century, the development of the automobile created a surge in demand for Thai rubber.

In the nineteenth century most of the Americans in Thailand were missionaries. They brought modern improvements which had profound economic implications: the printing press, medicine, and educational reforms. Americans were more readily accepted in the Thai court than Europeans because they seemed less interested in turning Thailand into a colony. The Thais had only to look east to French Indochina or west to British Burma and India to see what a future as an European colony would be like. American influence on the Thai economy would continue to modern times. But it would be interrupted by Japanese conquest in World War II and diminished by Japanese economic expansion in the postwar period.

The Role of Chinese

As Thailand slowly began to industrialize in the early nineteenth century, it was unable to meet the demand for tin, rubber, and other commodities because Thai farmers were unwilling to leave their rice-farming villages to work in distant mines and plantations. So Chinese laborers were imported to alleviate the labor shortage. By the end of the century development of the railroads was well under way. As in the United States, Chinese laborers were employed in the construction. As in the United States, many Chinese remained behind to live and work in the small towns which proliferated along the lines. These Chinese often started businesses and saved money while many Thai did not. In time, Chinese investors came to dominate Thailand's trade, finance, manufacturing, and mining.

In response to growing Chinese domination of the Thai economy in the 1930s, the government restricted immigration and required assimilation of Chinese already in Thailand. This policy was partly successful. Today there are many prominent business people who are native Thais. Yet, the Chinese are still prominent in international trade and banking. They have almost monopolized rice trading and gambling. But many have integrated so well into Thai society that it is often difficult to tell Chinese from Thai.

Japanese Influence

Due to Thailand's ability to straddle both sides, its economy emerged undamaged from World War II. Strong postwar demand sparked production of rice and timber; the nation prospered. The Japanese left in military defeat in 1945 but returned in economic victory in the 1960s; they have been the dominant foreign financial factor ever since.

Japan's natural resources are limited mainly to low-grade coal, waterpower, industrious people, and beautiful scenery. To survive it needs to draw on the resources of nations such as Thailand which possess rice, rubber, tin, iron ore, lumber, and sugar. Japan pays for these by selling cars, television sets, VCRs and other manufactured goods.

Japan invests massive amounts of capital in Thailand. The yen is now the dominant currency in the area. Japan's vital requirements for both the resources and use of the area's sea lanes will inevitably lead to increasing Japanese diplomatic and naval activity. Recent plans by Malaysia and Indonesia to nationalize the strategic Straits of Malacca represent an economic threat which cannot be ignored by Japan.

The Rise of Modern Industry

The Vietnam War was a benefit for Thailand's economy. The location of American air, logistic, and recreation facilities in Thailand provided a lift for the economy. Soon the nation went through waves of industrialization.

Agricultural processing was one of the first to modernize. In the 1970s and 1980s Dole and Mitsubishi invested in food canning, especially vegetables, pineapples, and various tropical fruits.

The next wave involved a surge in labor intensive industries such as textiles and shoes. This was followed by the development of capital intensive manufacturing such as petrochemicals and auto assembly. The current wave of economic development involves high technology, finance, and service industries.

These waves of modernization were fueled by considerable government and private borrowing, much of it from Japan. Foreign aid also played a role. In recent years Thailand has received aid from France, West Germany, and Britain. Some of these grants are designed to encourage trade with the sponsoring country.

5. *A Look at Thailand's Successful Economy*

Reason for Success

In recent years the Thai economy has been booming with seven to ten per cent growth per year. Bangkok is besieged with flocks of construction cranes which peck the earth from dawn to dusk. Troops of Japanese, packed with yen, search for good investments. Some economists are already calling Thailand the "fifth little dragon," after Korea, Hong Kong, Taiwan and Singapore.

Why is the Thai economy so successful? Thailand benefits because it is in the path of East Asia's low wage wave. Japan and the four little dragons long ago switched from labor to capital intensive industries; prosperity ended cheap labor. Many of their industries now seek cheap labor in Thailand. Within a decade the newly industrialized nations will probably include Indonesia, Bangladesh, and Sri Lanka. China and the Philippines will lag behind until they can resolve their political problems.

Successful efforts by the Thai government to attract foreign investments have contributed to the economy's success. Policies which generally favor free trade and foreign investment have attracted billions of dollars in the past twenty years. Japanese and American capital account for about half of it.

About ninety per cent of foreign investment is in manufacturing, trade, construction, oil drilling, and mining. Foreign subsidiaries in Thailand include such giants as Thai Shell, Toyota Motor Thailand, and Mitsubishi. Even indigenous companies, such as Siam Cement Group and the Metro Group, benefit from foreign investment in one way or another. Foreign money helped to create a new Thai entrepreneurial class, led by the Sophonpanich, Techapaibul, and Lamsam families.

In addition government policies seem designed to ensure minimum interference in the economy. In practice most government meddling is the result of haphazard coordination between government agencies and pay off demands by petty bureaucrats. Nevertheless, allocation of investments and determination of prices are left primarily to market forces.

Add to these Thailand's abundant natural resources, reasonably good infrastructure, and Bangkok's air and sea hubs, and you have the ingredients for a successful economic recipe.

Government Role in the Economy

Seven agencies develop, influence, and administer industrial policy. If you do business in Thailand, you will be involved with one or more of them. This is what they do. The National Economic and Social Development Board (NESDB) sets up a series of Five Year Plans which are designed to fill gaps and clean up problems created by private businesses rather than control them. Typical goals of Five Year Plans are improving fiscal policy, reducing balance of payment deficits, and improving infrastructure. It also develops industrial priorities, targets, and guidelines. The Board of Investment provides investment incentives. The Ministry of Commerce controls prices and international trade. The Bank of Thailand provides foreign exchange and special financing to selected industries and exporters. The Ministry of Industry issues factory licenses, zoning regulations, and industrial rules. The Industrial Finance Corporation issues long-term government credits to selected companies. Because these agencies sometimes have contradictory goals and policies, the Industrial Committee was created to coordinate them.

Infrastructure

Thailand has a good infrastructure consisting of electric power grids; air, sea, and land transport; telecommunications, and postal services. But all of these are becoming strained by the demands of a booming economy.

Sources of electrical energy include waterpower, oil, lignite, and natural gas. The country is trying to reduce its dependence on foreign oil. Thus there are opportunities for foreign companies involved in natural gas extraction, processing, and marketing.

Bangkok is the hub of the transportation system. Waterways still provide some transport of goods in and out of Bangkok, but roads and railways now carry most of the freight. The government-owned rail system, begun under King Chulalongkorn, is used mainly for long-distance shipment of bulk commodities such as rice, cement and crude oil. Before the railways it took weeks to transport cargo by boat or elephant to the north and northeast. Local transportation is by taxi, bus, or *samlor* (three-wheeled taxi). More and more Thais are purchasing cars.

Bangkok and the areas down river have major port facilities. Due to the boom major ports are clogged. Two new ports are being developed, one by a syndicate of foreign investors, including ARCO, at Laem Chabang.

The Thai Airways Company, government owned, provides domestic and regional service. The government has majority ownership in Thai Airways International; Scandinavian Airlines owns a minority share. The major international airport is Don Muang outside Bangkok.

Both phone and postal services are government owned. The phone system is not well developed by Western standards. There is only one telephone per hundred Thai. Only a quarter of the population has regular access to a telephone. Two-thirds of Thai telephones are allocated to business or government agencies. There should be good opportunities here for foreign telecommunications companies.

The government's priorities for improvement of the infrastructure include upgrading of rural roads, telecommunication systems, and airport traffic control systems; foreign companies will probably be involved.

Basic Industries

Thailand's first basic industries included agriculture and logging. Agriculture is still the foundation of the Thai economy. The central plain, which extends about three hundred miles north from the Gulf of Thailand, is one of the richest rice growing regions in the world. Thailand is the world's first rice producer and a major grower of tapioca, sugar cane, and corn. Thai farmers have been immensely successful because they keep bringing new land under cultivation and are willing to accept new technologies. Most Thai farmers are small landowners who work for themselves and are highly motivated. They watch the market carefully and are willing to shift from rice to other export crops such as cassava, mung beans, sorghum, tobacco, cotton, peanuts, cashew nuts, and soybeans. The success of Thai agriculture extends to forestry, fishery, and livestock.

Elephants furnished the initial source of power for logging. There are about 25,000 of them still in Thailand; most are employed in the forest industry. They study at Chiang Dao Technical School for Elephants for seven years and work for about sixty years after graduation. These elephants retire and die about the age of eighty. They have a strong union and work for only a few hours each morning; then they go for a dip in the nearest creek! In recent years Thailand has begun to reduce logging in order to preserve its dwindling forests.

Most of Thailand's mineral resources remain untouched, neither surveyed nor assessed. Thailand is rich in iron ore, tin and tungsten; manganese and marble; lead, limestone, and lignite; gypsum and garnet; rubies and rock salt; jade, quartz, and zinc. Thailand's tin industry has the romance of mining on the early American frontier featuring outlaws, claim jumping, false registration certificates, "lost" mines, and violent disputes.

Manufacturing is still mostly related to agricultural products: textiles, rubber, food, tobacco, and beverages. However, oil refining and high technology are rapidly developing. About forty per cent of Thailand's manufacturing is concentrated in the larger Bangkok area. This is due to the capital's central role in transportation, marketing, communications, and finance.

Trade

Thailand's main trading partners are Japan, the United States, Singapore, the Netherlands, Saudi Arabia, and the five other members of the Association of Southeast Asian Nations: Singapore, Malaysia, the Philippines, Indonesia, and Brunei.Thailand is one of the leading world exporters of rice, rubber, and tin; exports of teak, bauxite, sugar cane, tapioca, musk, cassava, tobacco, and tropical fruits are also considerable. About half of Thailand's petroleum consumption is imported.

Thailand is now an export-driven nation. But in the future increasing consumer spending will stimulate the manufacture of products for retail sale. This will create many new opportunities for American manufacturers of industrial equipment, machine tools, electrical machinery, electronic products, and consumer goods.

Banking and Stock Exchange

The Bank of Thailand, government owned, functions as the central bank, controls the money supply, foreign exchange, and the banking system. It has regularly devalued the baht to keep Thai exports competitive. At present the baht is linked to a basket of seven currencies in which the U.S. dollar receives the most weight.

The banking industry is highly concentrated. There are many government-owned banks but most are private. There is little competition. The fifteen largest banks compete for about ninety per cent of the business. This lack of competition stifles innovation. As an example almost all treasury bills and bonds are purchased by commercial banks which must hold them to maturity because there is no secondary market. Certificates of deposit do not exist, neither does commercial paper. Almost all business loans are restricted to the short term.

The Security Exchange of Thailand has a history of weak regulation and insider trading. After years of boom fueled by high margin, the stock market (in 1978 and 1990) plummeted. Yet there are good opportunities amid the chaos. Thailand's economy functions much like ours operated during the age of the robber barons.

One can buy Thai stocks directly, but there is much red tape and strict limits to foreign ownership in Thai companies. Quotas of stocks in large Thai companies allocated for foreign ownership fill quickly and sell at premiums. Most foreign investors interested in the Thai economy participate through the Thai Fund or the Bangkok Fund, regional international funds listed on major exchanges. The Thai stock market, like those in most booming economies, is very volatile; gains involving rapid price doubling and losses of more than a half in a few months are not unusual.

Labor, Research and Tourism

Some final comments needed to round out this brief discussion of the Thai economy involve the topics of labor, research, and tourism. All of these are important to growth.

Unions were legalized in 1972. Minimum wage laws were first introduced in 1973; they tend to lag inflation because they are normally not indexed to it. Some employers ignore labor laws. Labor costs are considerably less than those in Korea, Taiwan, Hong Kong, or Singapore.

The Asian Institute of Technology in Bangkok, operated by a consortium of Southeast Asian nations, is a key factor in Thailand's economic development. It is helping the nation improve its competitive position in semiconductor manufacturing, computer programming and software, and computer-aided design and manufacturing.

Tourism is still Thailand's major source of foreign exchange. More than five million tourists visit Thailand each year. They contribute over three billion dollars annually to the nation's economy, Thailand's largest source of foreign exchange.

Bangkok as a Regional Center

Southeast Asia is booming and Bangkok is emerging as its regional center. Changes are rampant. Soviet dominance of Vietnam disappeared with the Soviet Union. Vietnam, a nation with great natural resources, is now committed to a market economy; Japan is now its number one trading partner and buys eighty per cent of its oil. Vietnam is lowering tensions with China and improving its relations with the United States. The last time I flew in a civilian aircraft over Vietnam, in 1968, it drew anti-aircraft fire. In 1991 my Northwest Airlines flight serenely crossed the entire nation.

Nearby Singapore and Malaysia have had market economies for decades. The 1991 United Nations Cambodian Peace Plan has produced a rush of investment into Cambodia. Buses loaded with Japanese tourists now visit Angkor Wat and the Khmer Rouge killing fields. Except for some turmoil in East Timor and Burma, Southeast Asia is stable. Its economic and business prospects are probably better than they have ever been.

6. *Current Problems*

Problems of Success

Most of Thailand's problems are created by its booming success. The nation's population, industry, trade, and oil consumption are growing so rapidly that economic dislocations are inevitable. Thailand is plagued by environmental pollution, a stressed transportation grid, shortages of adequate housing, a lack of investment capital, and poor water and sewer services. The nation's unusual political stability has attracted refugees from nearby nations undergoing upheavals. Its export success has brought cries for protection from battered competitors. To top it off Thailand's freewheeling business environment has spawned a crippling corruption, once again verifying the assertion of the ancient Roman philosopher, Juvinal: "Prosperity is more brutal than war."

Population Problems

Since 1970 Thailand has had a policy of population control based on the slogan: "Many children make you poor." Through a program of family planning, population growth has been reduced from 3.4 per cent per annum in the 1960s to about 1.6 per cent at present, a reduction of about half. In spite of this success, many experts claim the population is still growing too rapidly. Unless there is better population control, resources which could be used to further productivity or expand exports will have to be used to provide more infrastructure for a growing population. Thailand now has more than fifty-nine million people. Roughly six million live in the Bangkok area. Half of all Thais are under the age of fifteen.

Jammed Infrastructure

Thailand's rapid economic growth has created considerable stress on the infrastructure. Transportation, communication, and energy networks cannot keep up with the requirements. The movement of exports, which have grown by about twelve per cent annually, sometimes exceed the capacities of Thailand's ports. This logjam is being resolved through construction and expansion of two deep seaports on the Gulf of Thailand. These include industrial estates, export processing facilities, and a highway to northeast Thailand bypassing Bangkok.

The increased use of electrical appliances, such as television sets and microwave ovens, will require about twenty per cent per year increases in electrical output. No one knows where it will come from. The International Monetary Fund is reluctant to support loans for fossil-burning power generation because of the pollution such plants produce. Bangkok is already covered with a blanket of smog.

Construction of skyscrapers in Bangkok goes on around the clock. At night the lighted movements of huge cranes makes the city look like it is infested by giant praying mantises. Developers make fortunes on construction and leave the problems of providing electricity, gas, roads, water, and sewers to the government. Only a few piers are in place for the new skytrain. Meanwhile it takes an hour to drive a mile in rush hour or rain. In Los Angeles traffic is stop-and-go; in Bangkok, it's just stop. Yet, two social services are in abundant supply: the military and the police.

Environmental Problems

As Bangkok's economy rises, the city itself sinks; the pumping of ground water has resulted in considerable land subsidence. Dead fish putrify on the surface of the Chao Phya River floating amid garbage and raw sewage. Many klongs, once graced with quaint sampans, are now filled with dirt, creating streets snarled with autos spewing noxious gases. On hot days the city's pumping stations are unable to satisfy water requirements; the resulting suction in the pipes pulls in polluted ground water, which is then distributed to household taps.

In the countryside rampant extraction of timber and mineral resources is destroying forests and damaging watersheds. Garbage from the cities is creating toxic dumps.

Both urban and rural pollution have concrete economic effects. Workers, sick from unhealthy air and water, are less productive. The charm of the Thai landscape which is disappearing may be an abstraction, but the tourists can sense it. Tourism may decline as it did in Singapore when it too "modernized." With it could go Thailand's major source of foreign exchange. Clean up of Thailand's abused environment could cost billions of bahts. Meanwhile the quality of life deteriorates for everyone.

Trade and Investment Problems

Thailand's trade and investment problems are so intricately intertwined they need to be covered as a single topic involving dependence on foreign oil, addiction to Japanese capital and American export markets, increasing foreign and domestic debt, and rising foreign protectionism.

Like the United States, Thailand imports about half its oil. Sharp increases in the international price of oil can cause big problems. The oil shock of 1973 increased Thailand's inflation to 24.3 per cent. Rising prices due to the 1990 Iraq crisis still reverberate through the economy. The government is trying to reduce this dependence by increasing the exploration and development of natural gas.

Rapid growth of the economy has caused an endless hunger for capital which has been fed mainly by Japanese financing. Thailand is so dependent upon Japanese capital that minor financial twitches in Tokyo can cause severe convulsions in Bangkok. When the Japanese stock market dropped in 1990, prices of Thai stocks plummeted. As a producer of agricultural commodities, Thailand has needed Japanese support during drops in world prices.

The Thai savings rate, though high by Western standards, falls far short of providing the capital needed for investment. Both the Thai government and businesses have to borrow heavily to make up the difference. This produces increasing budget deficits, periodic negative trade balances, over-leveraged businesses, and expanding interest costs for everyone. These conditions make Thailand particularly vulnerable to economic downturns. The use of fiscal and monetary policies to recover from recessions is made more difficult by the same conditions. Heavy indebtedness contributed to Thailand's deep recession in 1985-6.

Because its economy is export-driven, Thailand is especially vulnerable to protectionist legislation, particularly by the United States. The Thai government at times does not seem sensitive to American trade interests. In spite of a chronic American trade deficit with Thailand, the Thai government has protected the Thai Tobacco Monopoly by opposing legal import of cigarettes from the United States. Thai failure to honor many American copyrights and patents also feeds protectionist sentiments in the United States. If your industry involves publishing, pharmaceuticals, or software, you need to be especially wary.

Protectionism is rampant even among Thailand's closest trading partners. The Association of Southeast Asian Nations (ASEAN), founded in 1967 to reduce tariffs and improve trade, has had very limited success because members have not been able to overcome narrow national interests. Even without the threat of American protectionism, many Thai industries are extremely vulnerable to routine cyclical downturns in the American economy. For example, lower consumer spending in the United States can spell disaster for the Thai textile industry.

Rural Discontent

Thailand is not a nation of starving villagers, but there are wide disparities between standards of living in the cities and the countryside. The nation has never had peasant revolts, but they have happened in nearby countries. In the 1970s the communist Khmer Rouge in Cambodia turned the anger of impoverished rural people against the affluent population of the capital of Phnom Penh, seized and emptied the city, and created a holocaust. Such a process may have caused the abandonment of

Angkor Wat, another Cambodian capital in ancient times. Such events should not be ignored.

Annual per capita income in Bangkok is about $2700 but only about $900 in the countryside. Country people move to Bangkok to earn more money, avoid hard field work, and enjoy modern conveniences. In spite of such migrations to the lure of cities, seventy per cent of the Thai population still works the land.

These people suffer from many economic injustices. Loans by avaricious moneylenders carry interest rates up to one hundred per cent; this leaves few bahts for seed or farm machinery. Such punitive rates tend to restrict farm output and create resentments which can lead to political instability.

Unfortunately land tenancy seems to be increasing. Reliable figures are difficult to obtain, but probably ten to fifteen per cent of all Thai farmers are full tenants, meaning they own none of the land they till. Perhaps another twenty to thirty per cent are partial tenants who rent land in addition to what they own. These figures seem small, but in other parts of Asia such conditions have reduced motivation and caused considerable discontent. The problem of tenancy is exacerbated by the fact that many absentee landlords are speculators from Bangkok who have little or no empathy for the soil or those who till it.

This was not always the case. In Thailand's early days considerable empty land was available for farmers. By working a plot for only three years, a farmer obtained the right to use it. In 1874 King Chulalongkorn introduced the idea of individual land ownership. His reforms limited land ownership to an area a farmer could till himself or directly supervise. This wise decree made land tenancy rare and precluded the kind of exploitation which impeded agriculture in China and other parts of Asia during the same period.

In some areas, particularly the Golden Triangle in the north, the poverty of rural life is compensated for by opium growing. The Triangle, which is mostly in Burma and Laos, produces 750 tons of opium per year, satisfying half the world market. Competing armed factions, such as the Shan United Army (a vestige of the Nationalist Chinese Kuomingtang) and the Burmese Communist party, vie for control of production.

In the 1960s communist guerrillas in Thailand tried to marshal rural discontent, but their cruel atrocities caused loss of popular support. A Thai government amnesty program in the 1970s further weakened them. The present size and strength of the communist movement is probably small. But as long as incomes and living standards in the countryside lag those in the cities, there will be potential for trouble.

The Thai government is trying to alleviate urban-rural differences by expanding industrialization to the hinterlands. In the northeast the town of Buriram is benefiting from the presence of a Japanese wig manufacturer. Other manufacturing enclaves in the countryside include Lamphun Industrial Estate, just north of Ching Mai, and the northeastern city of Nakhon Ratchasima. These would be places to investigate for good factory sites. They are said to be available with reasonable prices, wage rates, and tax breaks.

Bureaucracy

Many American business people I spoke with in Thailand complained about government red tape, bureaucratic obsession with precise trivia, slow decisions, confusing regulations and tax laws, contradictory policies, fuzzy trade rules, and requests for bribes. Rules at the national level seem to be deliberately vague so each bureaucratic fiefdom can establish its own policies. This disparity in regulations and procedures can extend even to various offices in the same agencies. Such motley organization and patchwork administration facilitate arbitrary decisions, arcane paperwork procedures, political favoritism, and opportunities for bribes. To make matters worse, vague and arbitrary rules may sometimes be enforced with threats of fines or imprisonment.

Government functionaries use their low salaries as excuses for bribes, called "tea money." You may have to pay "tea money" to rent a car, avoid extra taxes, obtain legal benefits, rent or buy real estate, or get a child entered in a good school. These practices, though somewhat traditional in Asia, impede the development of a modern, free market economy. They make it difficult to account for the true cost of any goods or services. Business assets, including time, cannot be allocated efficiently. The true loyalty of employees and agents remains in doubt. Modern systems of accounting, management, marketing, finance, and information transmission cannot be used effectively.

The reach of Thai governmental bureaucracy extends to control of government-owned businesses. Thailand has about two hundred state-owned businesses varying in size and by industry. Government control varies from full ownership to small interests. Many of these companies are too small to be efficient. Employment is often based on favoritism rather than skills. Wages for state-owned enterprises are fifty per cent higher than for private companies. Most of these concerns are protected, in one way or another, from free market competition. Their goals and operations often respond to government rather than market pressures.

In addition to owning many businesses, the Thai government has a policy of protecting infant private industries. This is probably a mistake. The theory is good; a nation closes its borders to imports which threaten inchoate industries until they grow enough to compete. But in practice infant industries which are protected too long become too dependent upon protection. These hothouse lilies seldom develop the ability to compete on world markets. They often require excessive purchase of foreign machine tools and industrial commodities thus adding to the loss of foreign exchange. This effect is the exact opposite of the original intention.

Ethnic Divisions

Thailand's ethnic divisions fall into two categories: indigenous minorities and refugees.

By far the largest indigenous minority is the Chinese. Although the Thai originally came from China and the royal family has Chinese blood, the modern influx of Chinese began about 1900. They came as construction workers for canals and railroads, worked hard, saved money, and became affluent. As they gained economic power, they resisted government control developing their own schools and social service agencies. Chinese merchants kept their ledgers in Chinese to make taxation more difficult.

In 1910 the Thai government tightened taxation of the Chinese. The Chinese business community retaliated with a three-day strike which stopped most Thai commerce. The Chinese Chamber of Commerce which was founded about this time still exists today.

In the late 1930s the Thai government reacted to growing Chinese domination of the economy by imposing severe restrictions on Chinese schools, businesses, and newspapers. Many Chinese were forced to assimilate and take Thai names.

When the Japanese occupied Thailand during World War II, they brutalized the Chinese and used them as slave laborers to build the "railroad of death" to Burma. Shortly after the war ended, Bangkok exploded in the nine-day Chinese riot of September, 1945. Four years later the communist conquest of China divided many Thai Chinese into communist and nationalist supporters.

The Thai are quite tolerant people and the Chinese are now more assimilated. But some potential for ethnic problems remains. The Chinese now number four million. They still have such economic power that Thai say "the more Chinese blood, the more success."

There are many other minority groups in Thailand beside the Chinese. There are more Laos in northeastern Thailand than in Laos itself. Much of the culture of northern Thailand is Khmer, of Cambodian origin. In the far north the incursion of Chinese hill tribes has complicated the cultural mix.

The problem of ethnic minorities has been made more difficult by the influx of refugees from recent wars in Vietnam, Cambodia, and Laos. Each new upheaval brought a new throng: Laos, Khmer, Hmong, Vietnamese, and others. Most settled in crowded camps along Thailand's disputed and poorly marked borders. In recent years there have been as many as half a million refugees in these camps. Some have now returned to their mother countries to participate in internecine conflicts. Others, including women and children, have been attacked in their camps by Cambodian forces and local bandits. All have created military and financial strains on the Thai government which have only partially been ameliorated by international aid.

Burmese Insurgency

Thailand has a long border with Burma which is now in turmoil. Although 1991 Nobel peace laureate Aung San Suu Kyi has been under house arrest since July 1989, her Burmese Democratic League won the May 1990 election in a landslide. Since the Burmese junta has refused to cede power, Kyi supporters have set up a "Kyi Trail" to transport weapons purchased from the Khmer Rouge in Cambodia across Thailand to Burma. Thai forces have moved to interdict these shipments, and there have been a number of firefights. If such clashes continue and increase, they could have a negative effect on tourist travel north of Bangkok.

7. *Doing Business with the Thais*

Opportunities

Some of the best business opportunities in Thailand involve manufacturing and sales of medical and telecommunications equipment, avionics and ground support systems; food processing, packing, and refrigeration; computers, construction, consumer products, chemicals, energy, drugs, and plastic production machinery. Agricultural opportunities include dairy production, cotton, tobacco, wheat, apples, pig and rabbit breeding, and slaughterhouses.

Over seven hundred American companies have invested in Thailand. Most have been very successful. Returns on investment can be very high, especially where joint investment with a Thai partner is involved. Estimated growth rates for the industries just mentioned range from ten per cent for food processing machinery to thirty per cent for computers.

Again, the information in this book should be used as a general guide. Much of it may be out of date by the time you read this. You can receive updates on the latest changes in opportunities, regulations, and procedures by contacting the agencies listed in the chapter on "Useful Addresses." Questions of a legal nature should be directed to your corporate attorney or local lawyers.

Financing

The Bank of Thailand acts as the central bank by providing credit and regulating reserves to commercial banks. It is also the government's own bank. The number, size, and operations of foreign banks are severely restricted. Thai banks account for about three-quarters of all credit extended in Thailand. Foreign banks tend to circumvent Thai banking restrictions through major shareholdings in Thai finance companies.

The official Thai financial system is conservative, circumspect, and limited in its services. Domestic credit is restricted and foreign borrowing is discouraged by a tax on interest remitted abroad. Yet, foreign borrowing continues at such a rate that Thai interest rates are largely determined by foreign lenders. Small businesses and people with moderate incomes are often unable to find adequate credit through normal channels. Consequently there is a vast informal credit market ranging from finance companies to pawn shops. But even on the informal market little long-term or medium-term credit is available. Most credit, official and informal, is short-term. Interest rates can run from eighteen per cent to eighty-four per cent. The uncontrolled expansion of informal credit markets has led, in the past decade, to chaotic interest rates, speculative tremors, staggering insolvencies, and collapsed pyramid schemes.

Here again the government exerts an influence. Projects with high official priorities may obtain ten-year loans from the Industrial Finance Corporation at reasonable rates.

Establishing a Business

Thailand recognizes seven structures for businesses: public limited company, private limited company, limited partnership, registered ordinary partnership, unregistered ordinary partnership, sole proprietorship, and branches of foreign companies.

Rules for public limited companies seem stringent. There must be at least one hundred shareholders. Half the capital must be controlled by physical persons each of whom may not own 0.6 per cent of the total. Other shareholders must not exceed ten per cent each. As a result of these constraints most foreign investors set up *private* limited companies.

Subsidiaries and branch offices each have advantages. Branch offices receive more favorable tax treatment on repatriated profits than subsidiaries. But it is easier for subsidiaries to obtain licenses, deal with bureaucrats, administer themselves, change managers, and act as legal entities.

To form a Thai limited company at least twenty-five per cent of the capital must be paid in cash and be guaranteed by a bank. The rest of the shares may be allotted for services or property. At each dividend distribution at least five per cent of after-tax profits must be allocated to a reserve fund until such fund equals ten per cent of capital. There must be at least seven founders to form a Thai limited company. One of the seven must be a Thai resident or an alien with a resident visa; this director must be authorized to bind the company. There are additional restrictions for companies coming under the Alien Business Law.

Shares may be common or preferred and vary in the number of votes and rights to dividends. But non-voting shares are not allowed. Par value must be at least five baht. Certificates may be nominal or bearer (if fully paid). No treasury stock is allowed.

Do not act on the basis of the above information alone; it is sure to change. But it should furnish some guidance and help you frame questions. You might begin by testing your business concept with a Thai agent or intermediary. You should obtain both American and Thai legal advice. Then check government and private agencies listed in the chapter on "Getting Help." If the prospects look favorable at this time, you might consider opening an operation in Thailand.

Role of the Government

Although official Thai policy supports business, the Thai bureaucracy sometimes makes the conduct of business difficult. The various Thai government agencies which have been described have different responsibilities, but they all function in the same way: slowly and arbitrarily, with compulsive attention to precise trivia. For example, tariff rules involving the routine import of samples and promotional literature (which are never items for sale) are complex involving detailed inventory, multiple reports, and invoices denominated in foreign currency. "Gifts" may be required. Bribes, called "eating," are common. They are usually widely shared. Check with your corporate attorney to be sure you do not violate American law.

A British electronics executive told me he found it easier to pay a small amount of "tea money" than to have his samples "processed." "It was better," he said, "to pay the paper monster than to get caught in his jaws. For once it has a taste of your reports, its appetite becomes endless." An American oil manager was more blunt: "Corruption here is as common as orchids."

Thai government bureaucracies, like their commercial counterparts, are administered by a *saraban,* a special section which shepherds endless flows of paper up and down long hierarchical ladders. Each *saraban* keeps detailed records of the location and progress of every scrap of paper. The wheels of this special clearing and routing center grind slowly, but beware of bypassing a *saraban*. Memos, such as informal notes, which are not registered with the *saraban*, disappear; they pass on to a paperwork nirvana. For each department maintains its own bureaucratic rituals and forsakes all others.

Investment Laws and Regulations

The following information is derived from material supplied by the government of Thailand; it is subject to change. It is best to write or call the agencies listed in the chapter titled "Useful Addresses."

The Ministry of Education controls factory establishment licenses. Priority is granted to investments in special zones designated by the Industrial State Authority. Authorization to start production anywhere in Thailand must be obtained from the Office of National Environment. New factories in or near Bangkok are discouraged due to congestion and pollution. Once your factory is in operation it must be registered at the Department of Commercial Registration (at the Ministry of Trade) and the Revenue Department (at the Ministry of Finance). With some exceptions foreigners are not allowed direct ownership of buildings and land; projects in special industrial zones are usually exempt from this rule. The prime minister of Thailand is president of the Board of Investment, which is responsible for coordinating and centralizing all government agency approvals for all investments in Thailand.

Your project is more likely to be approved if it is located in an industrial estate, uses local raw materials and labor, has a large Thai ownership, is environmentally clean, and results in increased Thai exports. It is less likely to be approved if it has little Thai ownership, uses many imported materials, competes with many Thai businesses in Thai markets, and operates in an industry which is already heavily subsidized by the Thai government. Application procedures usually take about six months.

Under certain circumstances the Thai government, through the Board of Investment, offers guarantees against new domestic or foreign competition, nationalization, competition from government-owned firms, and controls of export prices. Other incentives may include tax holidays; approval to buy land, repatriate foreign currency, or bring in special technicians; or exemption from duties on import of machinery and raw materials. You have to cut your own deal.

The government requires a majority Thai ownership in businesses engaged in rice farming, real estate sales, mining, law, architecture, building construction, and other designated industries. Some foreign investors circumvent this requirement by involving a "sleeping partner," such as a Thai bank, or diluting the fifty-one per cent Thai capital among so many shareholders that all cannot be actively engaged in policy. The requirement for Thai majority ownership is waived where businesses are involved in areas considered critical by government planners or where no Thai capital is available.

Tax Laws

According to stated Thai government policies tax laws are designed to encourage foreign investment in priority areas stated in the National Plan. Corporations operating in industries or locations not designated for incentives pay relatively high taxes. Due to chronic high budget deficits the Thai government has increased taxes regularly since 1984. Tax rates on interest earnings were increased, a new estate tax was imposed, the standard deduction for self-employed was reduced, and favorable rates for companies listed on the stock exchange were abolished. Income tax rates, now about forty per cent, are considered to be higher than any other Southeast Asian nation except Malaysia. Transaction taxes vary by industry but can also be forty per cent. A variety of fees are levied on ownership and transfer of capital. The capital gains tax for non-residents at this time is twenty-five per cent. Personal rates now top at sixty-five per cent. Indirect taxes are plethoric, high, and ubiquitous. Subsidiaries are taxed on income from all sources regardless of origin. Branches are taxed only on revenue originating in Thailand. In both cases international tax agreements take precedence.

No Thai politician has ever run for office on a platform of "no new taxes." Consequently Thai businesses do not try to read lips. They simply cheat; tax fraud is rampant.

Thai accountants are needed to minimize taxes and ensure nominal compliance with the latest government regulations; these are promulgated by the Thai Revenue Department. Books for Thai limited companies must be available in the Thai language for tax authorities to peruse. Annual reports and balance sheets must be issued yearly and incorporated in the minutes of the annual meetings.

Special Zones

The Industrial Estate Authority has designated four regions as Investment Promotion Zones: Songkla, Nakon Ratchasima/Saraburi, Khon Kaen, and Chiang Mai/Tak/Lampoon. Companies locating in these zones may qualify for special subsidies such as lower sales taxes, exemptions from corporate taxes, and tax breaks on development expenses such as installation of utilities. Companies exporting at least half of their production may qualify for waivers of import and export customs duties and partial exemptions of income tax in proportion to the value of their exports. Limited companies in Investment Promotion Zones may also own land.

In addition to Investment Promotion Zones, industrial estates have been established near the port of Bangkok, at Lard Krabang (for export processing), Khon Kaen (for natural gas production), Kampaengpetch/Nakom Ratchasima (for chemical industries), and Nakhon Sawan (for agro-food). Others are being developed.

Business Organizations

Thai business organizations, like Thai government bureaucracies, are vertical, hierarchical systems designed to fulfill cultural needs for authority and conformity. Functional areas such as management, finance, accounting, and marketing operate as separate fiefdoms with poor cross-communication. This often results in conflicting policies and procedures, gaps and duplications. There is little or no delegation of responsibility. Most problems are passed up the ladder for solution by the only person expected to know all aspects of the company's operation, the top boss. Links between the vertical chain are based on the patron system. The patron, a superior, provides protection, influence, and favors. The client, a subordinate, provides services and personal loyalty to the patron. A powerful patron may have several clients, but a client has only one patron. This system, originally social, was modified for Thai business and politics.

Managing Employees

Business is a social activity which is deeply rooted in Thai culture. At its heart Thailand is hierarchical, so are its management concepts. The system goes back to the fifteenth century and involves, not just royalty, but everyone in Thai society. There are hundreds of terms of address based upon subtle differences in status. One's social status is accepted because it is considered to be a result of merit earned or not earned in a previous life. As an executive you need to understand the Thai system of hierarchies and operate within it.

Unlike Americans, Thai of lower status, such as waiters and cabbies, do not call people of higher status "pal" or "buddy." Nor do they offer unsolicited opinions. Indeed, as a manager, you may not be able to get *any opinions at all.*

King Ram Khamhaeng in the thirteenth century hung a huge bell near the palace to be rung by anyone who wanted to discuss a problem with the king. It was the most silent bell in Thailand and was eventually removed. Like King Ram Khamhaeng, it will do you no good to "keep your office door open." You will discover what is going on only by going out.

Although the relationship between superior and subordinate in Thai management practice is formal and authoritarian, the boss is expected to be benevolent and paternalistic. He or she will spend much time at employees' weddings, birthday parties, and family funerals. Since workers are considered junior members of the corporate family, few are fired. In contrast the American system features an easygoing egalitarian relationship involving first-name rapport and good-humored patter. But there is little benevolence. American employees are fired in the same glib, mechanical way. An American food-processing manager told me the best way to handle Thai employees was to be sincerely interested in them and their families, socialize outside business hours, listen patiently, criticize privately, train carefully, use intermediaries to save face, and fire only as a last resort. Above all, show respect for your employees.

Concept of Work

For many Americans work is at the center of their identities. They think and talk work in their private lives. In contrast many Thais consider their personal lives to be the center of their identities and think and talk about their personal lives when on the job. Americans will draw a sharp distinction between work time and fun time; Thais do not. They work at play and play at work. Thais expect work to be fun and may drift away from a new project as soon as the novelty wears off. They expect time off during working hours to run errands and socialize. This attitude is rooted in Thailand's rural beginnings where such important economic activities as plowing, planting, harvesting, and rice threshing were accompanied by festivals featuring song, wine, courtship, and parties. The industrialization of Thailand has been so recent that most city workers are still country folk at heart.

Since a Thai person's place in life has already been determined by his or her *karma* (store of merits and demerits from a previous life), it is difficult for a manager to instill a spirit of ambition or competitiveness. Thais will work hard when the benefit is obvious and immediate but will seldom work extra hard for deferred rewards. Impersonal quantitative methods of control, such as management by objectives, seldom work in a Thai business environment because Thais view work as a social function. They want such warm personal relationships between people that even the phone may be viewed as too mechanical. For a Thai there is no such thing as "talking business" objectively. They take criticism personally. Nor do they like to be regimented by such mechanical devices as business schedules, spreadsheets, itineraries, daily plans, inventory forms, payroll print-outs, and balance sheets, which they call "mother's lists."

Labor Laws

Thai labor laws are very cursory. They seem to be in a constant state of flux and enforcement is desultory. Labor unions are weak and strikes are rare. Labor need not be represented on boards of directors or management committees. A firm's relationship with its employees is governed more by custom then by law. Thais do not work efficiently unless happy with the work situation.

Most Thai companies contribute to an insurance fund which covers employee sickness and accidents. Employees receive special compensation upon termination. Large companies and foreign firms often offer wages in excess of the legal minimum, meals at low prices, housing and medical benefits, low cost loans, and retirement benefits. It is the custom for businesses to grant young men one-time leaves of two or three months to serve as monks. Workers from agricultural areas are usually allowed to return home to help with the harvests.

Though workers rarely strike, they petition management to resolve labor problems. Since they dislike discord, you must assume petition problems are major and take them seriously.

Training, Hiring, and Firing

Thailand's low-wage labor requires expensive training. Without it the nation's products would be too poor in quality to export. Japanese businesses in Thailand particularly recognize the importance of investing in people. Both cultural and technical training programs are facilitated by the traditional Thai respect for teachers and learning.

Hiring, firing, promotion, and demotion are complicated by the social and cultural aspects of Thai business life. American companies have some unique advantages to offer potential Thai employees: opportunities for overseas training; higher wages, salaries, and benefits; chances to learn modern technologies, an English-speaking environment, and promotion based on performance rather than connections. Yet some Thais are reluctant to work for American companies because they feel Americans are quicker to fire workers, reserve top jobs for Americans, and have more stringent work rules. So you should look for Thai applicants who will appreciate the advantages and be able to handle the disadvantages. You may find yourself hiring families and groups of relatives; this is a normal way of doing business. Unfortunately, termination of an employee may result in such a loss of "face" that his or her family, friends, and relatives (who may comprise most of your work force) will also leave. You should consider the social aspects of promotion and demotion. If necessary to demote an employee, it may be best to give him or her a face-saving title, such as "prince of the floors."

There are ways to avoid loss of face by criticizing indirectly. Try using hypothetical examples for real situations, introducing an old procedure as new, and framing criticism as suggestions. Work groups are a Thai tradition which allows criticism to be directed at the group rather than the individual.

Thais tend to be loyal to the boss rather than the company. In tradition promotion is achieved by deference, respect, and loyalty to one's superior. This system is slowly changing to a more impersonal system based on rewards for achievements, hard work, and diligence.

Problem Solving and Decision Making

For Thai people problems can threaten the social fabric. They can result in embarrassing confrontations. Whoever is at fault may lose face. In the Thai system one who finds a problem may become one. So Thai workers often hide problems. A good manager will find ways for employees to find and resolve problems anonymously or automatically. These might involve suggestion boxes, computer or mechanical checks, or ways for an employee to identify a problem symbolically or "accidentally."

The American system of decision making tries to be objective, uses statistics, and sets deadlines to conserve valuable time. Though many people may give technical advice, the final decision is often made by the executive in charge. In contrast Thai business people will often delay a decision until the problem resolves itself. Decision making may cause disagreements and confrontations. No one wants to be personally responsible so differences may be glossed over in attempts to reach a consensus. Though this may involve lengthy discussions, the Thai would rather lose time than face. Even problems sent up to higher authority may come back down unresolved.

For Thais open criticism is seen as a form of violence because it destroys social peace and harmony. You will likely hear an open opposing point of view only when an employee has decided to leave for another company. Then he may rip you and your operation with rare frankness and sharply edged criticism.

Once a decision has been made, it may be difficult to implement. Most Thai people are not willing to be led too far too fast. They might show support for new decisions but quietly ignore their requirements.

A Land of Opportunity

Doing business with the Thais probably involves more opportunities than problems. According to U.S. Department of Commerce's "Foreign Economic Trends" for Thailand dated July 1991, "U.S. investors established here are almost without exception enthusiastic about their operations in Thailand and are reinvesting heavily." In some cases American companies have beaten Japanese competition. Colgate-Palmolive has taken over almost half of the Thai shampoo market once controlled by the Japanese.

8. Bargaining

Preparation

Each bargaining situation is different. Some of the following ideas might fit your needs.

Your first steps in preparing for negotiations with Thais will be similar to those used to prepare for negotiations with Americans. Make sure your Thai counterparts have bargaining authority. Establish your walkaway point early. Understand and identify the goals of both sides. Identify common ground and prepare a list of concessions you can offer without injuring your interests. Discuss the bargaining process with colleagues who have been through it.

Reserve the first day or two after your arrival in Thailand for rest. Prepare a proposed agenda and a list of facilities you would like to visit. You may need to plan for several trips and determine goals for each. Confirm appointments and reservations several times. The phone can be a good tool for preparation. AT&T Language Line Service provides excellent translators for international phone conversations.

A smart negotiator starts bargaining before the other side knows it is involved. So kick off the ball before they are aware the game has started! Quietly gather information about your Thai counterparts and their companies. Investigate market systems, prices, and technical considerations. Explore possibilities *informally* with appropriate agencies of the Thai government. They will be easier to deal with when your questions seem hypothetical and they are not immediately pushed for decisions. Such off the record negotiations can be far more important than formal applications, which should be the *end* of negotiations rather than the beginning.

Organizing the Negotiating Team

The composition of your negotiating team will vary depending upon the situation. Never negotiate alone; you will need to divide the speaking and listening roles. Your speaker will usually be the senior member of your team. The listener/recorder should be someone who is extremely sensitive to the nuances of symbolic and non-verbal communication. Your team will probably also need an interpreter, technical expert, and someone to run errands, such as arranging reservations. If you plan to set up an operation in Thailand after the close of the deal, your senior team member would be the ideal person to run it; the deal will hold up better if the senior person who negotiated it is on the scene. Another team member could be designated as home office liaison for your Thai operation.

Someone should be assigned responsibility for bringing materials. These will range from typewriters to business cards printed in Thai. You may need to bring small computers, copy paper and ink, flip charts; movie, slide, or overhead projectors; electrical adapters, transformers, or converters; VCRs, cassettes, or cameras. Software for computer translations is available from Pacific Rim Connections, Inc. of Burlingame, California.

Stereotypes and Language Problems

Thai business people are familiar with Americans. Since the end of World War II, the United States has provided Thailand with well over a billion dollars in grants and loans. Today the United States is the largest market for Thai exports and over ten thousand Thai students attend American colleges.

Yet many stereotypes remain. For some Americans these involve impressions of Siamese twins, Siamese cats, and *Anna and the King of Siam*. (Anna was Mrs. Anna Leonowens, a teacher at King Mongkut's court in the 1860s, whose very imaginative memoirs led Westerners to view Thais as distorted stereotypes.)

Thai stereotypes of foreigners, called *farang* in Thai, center on visions of tall, hairy, meat-smelling people, who confuse technical competence with wisdom and miss the lofty parts of life because their heads are usually bowed in order to keep their eyes on the bottom line.

The problems of stereotyping are compounded by language difficulties. A Japanese electronics executive I met at the Ministry of Finance posed a riddle: "A person who speaks several languages is called multi-lingual. What do you call a person who speaks only one language?" The answer: "An American." Sad, but true. Most Americans are denied entrance to much of the Thai culture because they speak no Thai. Languages provide hosts of nuances, code words, and culturally derived connotations which are deeply significant for the intricate process of cross-cultural bargaining. In the lexicon of your counterpart's language "fairness" may mean preferential prices for old friends, not equal opportunities for all. "I will make an effort" may mean a polite rejection. One may wait for all eternity for something promised "soon." At least a fourth of the meanings of all ideas passing between languages may be lost due to differences in syntax, grammar, honorifics, connotations, and interpreters. Only one who has taken the time and trouble to learn Thai can belong to the group which best benefits from its use.

Intermediaries

Since personal relationships with Thai counterparts may take some time to develop, it may be best to start with a local independent agent who already has contacts. Such agents may be contacted through banks, government trade organizations in Thailand, U.S. agencies (such as the Commerce Department), the American Chamber of Commerce in Thailand, or your own trade association. Criteria for selecting agents include the number and quality of the agent's contacts, evaluation of recommendations, and types of product lines. The product lines the agent already carries should be similar but not competitive with yours. Agents who speak Thai are necessary to obtain widespread acceptance of consumer goods.

You should probably consider intermediaries other than independent agents. These could include prime contractors, licensees, franchisees, distributors, and joint venture partners. If you are a medium or small-size American exporter, you might not get sufficient attention from a large Thai importer or distributor. Consider a smaller, more specialized Thai importer which has a good track record of handling products like yours.

Your success will depend largely on how well you support your agent or intermediary. You must validate yourself and your firm to this person so he or she can validate you to potential customers. This will require solid support such as strong financial, informational, and technical back-up; rapid reaction to customer problems, and the field presence of top management. You will have to be very visible, helpful, creditable, and patient. As your business develops, you may wish to replace your agent or intermediary with an employee. The first job offer might be to your agent or intermediary.

Getting to Know You - Protocol and Entertaining

Your Thai counterparts will insist on knowing you well. They will want to become familiar with you, your company, and the lines of authority within it. Personal relationships will have to be developed before any business can be conducted.

You might begin the process of "getting to know you" by asking your Thai counterparts to visit your office or factory in the United States. If they accept you will be at an advantage; let them deal with strange customs, foods, and languages rather than you! Cultural shock will then work for your side.

If your Thai counterparts are unable to visit you in the United States, you might decide to make a video of your plant or office. The video could include interviews with key employees and information about your company's goals, standards, and products. Be sure to bring your own VCR to Thailand since Asian PAL VCRs do not take VHS or Beta cassettes. Your video, combined with letters of recommendation from banks, government officials, and mutual business acquaintances, should provide a good first impression. You should ask for similar credentials from your counterpart.

Thai protocol begins and ends with smiles which are particularly effusive in Thailand. So be gushy. Sometimes the traditional *wai* may be rendered. Always return it by putting your hands, prayer like, on your chest, and bowing slightly. You can use *wai* to say hello, goodby, sorry, and thank you.

Due to the hierarchical nature of Thai society, introductions can be a problem. One must offer the proper verbal and non-verbal signs of respect. But respect for whom? While American status is based on occupation and earnings, Thai status is often related more to earned religious merit, government position, education, age, and place in one's family. It is important, therefore, to gather much information on people before you meet them.

Unlike the Chinese Thai introduce by first name, preceded with a title such as *Khun* (Mr., Mrs., Ms.), *Nai* (businessman), or *Tahn* (dignitary or monk). Use of the first name is formal and not considered familiar as in the West.

When introduced stand up and present your business card so it can be read by the recipient. Your hotel can arrange to have the reverse side printed in Thai. (Treat business cards with respect.)

The process of "getting to know you" will entail considerable socializing and entertaining. This may take the form of meals, drinks, sports, or other forms of entertainment. Thais enjoy parties where everyone enjoys the fun. Games, songs, and food are important. This is not the time for one-on-one discussions of Immanuel Kant or self-serving soliloquies. So skip the monologue.

Etiquette for visits to Thai homes was covered in Chapter Two. Addresses of suitable restaurants for business entertainment are listed in Chapter Thirteen. Do not start to consume food or beverages until asked by your host. If not asked, wait until your host starts to eat. Thai people eat with a spoon in the right hand; the fork, in the left hand, is used to push food on the spoon. Knives are seldom used because food is served in small bits. The host serves the guests. When finished, leave the fork and spoon and a small dab of food on the plate to show you had enough to eat.

For calls on your Thai counterparts which do not involve meals, tea or coffee may be served to signify it is time to leave. If you follow the American custom of serving a beverage as soon as a guest arrives, you may end the visit prematurely!

Throughout the process of "getting to know you," small, thoughtful gifts are in order. Suitable examples include prestige brands of alcohol, tobacco, and toiletries. Thais do not usually acknowledge gifts sent by mail or messenger. So deliver them in person. Gifts must always be wrapped beautifully. When receiving a gift set the gift aside to open later. Never return or refuse a gift or mention its value.

Concepts of Time

American time references include "time-frames," "points in time," and "windows of time." "Time is money" which can be "saved" or "wasted." Time is so precious it is sliced into small bits and placed in schedules. Americans only "go around once," with impatient gusto.

All this is nonsense to Thai people. Time for the Thai is circular and slower. For them, watches do not "run," they "walk." Days, seasons, years, even human lives, bend back on themselves in inevitable and interminable cycles. Why rush when time is infinite? It is easy to have patience when time never "runs out."

This difference in attitude towards time represents an important factor in the bargaining process.

Secrecy

When bargaining it is important to respect the confidentiality of negotiations with your Thai counterpart. Terms and conditions can be much more flexible when negotiations are secret, particularly in Thailand where negotiators may "lose face" over every concession. Without publicity tacit understandings may be more easily withdrawn or restated. An issue delayed for later consideration in private need not be brought up again if things go your way; if they do not, you will be free to do so. Your Thai counterparts will also be more willing to discuss their problems if they are not made public.

Bargaining Motivation

Before beginning bargaining try to analyze your Thai counterpart's goals and motivation. These will usually be complex and subtle. Prices and profits may not be as important as they are to you. The other side will likely be more motivated by concern for quality, a need for a reliable source of supplies, a desire for effective foreign distribution, technical or training assistance, or requirements to conform with Thai government policies. You will likely benefit more in the long run by establishing a win-win situation (with enforceable guarantees) than trying to gain a quick short-term advantage.

You will probably be under greater time pressure than your Thai counterpart because your company will likely want increased profits every quarter to impress stockholders, the corporate version of "I want it all now." Your counterpart may be more concerned with gaining market share and contributing to Thailand's long-term expansion of exports. Like many Asians, Thais can think in decades, even generations.

Bargaining Behavior

American and Thai behavior in the negotiating process is very different. Americans are very direct; Thais, indirect and subtle. Americans usually want "to get down to business" immediately; Thais want to socialize first. Americans can be compulsive about logic, facts, and precise figures; Thais are more concerned with human relationships and general goals.

In some ways you should match Thai behavior. Sensitivity to others is a basis for civilized society. Emphasize decorum and dress conservatively in subdued colors. Do not be frank. The back bayous of Bangkok are figuratively filled with the business bones of foreign business executives who were frank. In Thailand a little fabricated flattery works wonders; so do as the Thais.

Westerners accept honest show of emotion. But with Thais you must be restrained. Never show anger. It is considered extremely rude to "vent steam." It will quickly destroy your business relationship. Only a smiling serene demeanor is acceptable. That way everyone saves "face."

An English construction engineer told me the Thai refused to fulfill his firm's multi-million dollar contract because a low-level member of the Thai negotiating team had been inadvertently slighted by a member of the British team: "If you slight one Thai team member you slight them all. Europeans and Americans know negotiations will be difficult, and a few egos will be bruised, but they also know they will salve the pain by getting together for drinks afterwards. Thais will take a frown or tone of voice as a giveaway slight and may quickly seek revenge."

Potential for Misunderstanding

There is great potential for misunderstanding in negotiating with Thais. Thais are not assertive. They seldom initiate, propose, persuade, or contradict others. Because Thais mask their feelings you may wrongly conclude they have the same goals and motivation as you. They, like you, will often be guided by subconscious assumptions which lead them to distort the facts.

Misunderstandings will occur even in such simple functions as dealing with servants or organizing a business event. You can minimize misunderstandings by asking your Thai counterparts to confirm communications in both Thai and English.

Limiting Risks

If you plan to manufacture in Thailand consider beginning with a final assembly operation and delay full production and technology transfer until you have the inevitable problems worked out.

Be wary of extending too much credit. Particularly when competing with Japanese, it will be difficult to overcome credit cost competition. Thailand is a credit-poor country with high interest rates. The Japanese, due to their high savings rate, can offer credit at relatively low rates. It is difficult to compete with this combination. You might circumvent this problem by arranging a countertrade deal.

Be wary of unexpected gifts or concessions, especially those related to opportunities to share costs. They could become "white elephants" which you can ill afford.

In bargaining be careful about technology transfers. In Thailand trademarks may be registered for successive ten-year periods. Patents are granted for fifteen years. Neither do much good. Counterfeiting is widespread, particularly for proprietary drugs. Many firms advertise warnings concerning counterfeits of their products. Be sure you bargain for a guaranteed way to ensure the protection of your technology.

You can also limit risk by writing the contract to include an initial period in which either party may cancel it. Avoid agreeing to contracts which are longer than needed.

Coming to Agreement

During the bargaining process you must continue to build personal relationships with your Thai counterparts. A deal seldom is sealed suddenly. As friendships develop agreements will also develop. Like dots of paint on an impressionistic canvas, your little discussions will gradually assume meaningful shapes. When everyone sees the same picture, it will be time to draw up a detailed agreement. The Thai decisions will have been made elsewhere, not at the negotiating meetings. They use such meetings primarily to gather information on such topics as your technical capabilities, product costs, and quality control. They may treat you as a tutor rather than as a potential partner.

The Contract

In general contracts are respected in Thailand. However, your Thai counterparts may feel free to renegotiate the contract when conditions change or as soon as your team has left the country. That is why it might be a good idea to assign your chief negotiator as chief executive officer of your new Thai operation.

Details such as agents' commissions, sales prices, delivery dates, financing, and means and times of payment should be clearly stated. Try to anticipate changing circumstances and arrange a contract with sufficient flexibility.

9. How to Get Help

Need for Help

There are roughly 350,000 manufacturing firms in the United States. Few of these export. As a result U.S. exports represent only about eight per cent of its gross national product, about a third the percentage of other nations.

Many American firms seem to be reluctant to use the help which is available from our government. Perhaps they fear red tape. Yet the services provided by the U.S. government are timely, thoroughly researched, effective, and often free.

Sources of help include U.S. government agencies, private U.S. government organizations, and a variety of Thai organizations. Addresses for many of these are located in Chapter Thirteen.

U.S. GOVERNMENT AGENCIES

The International Trade Administration

The International Trade Administration, an agency of the Department of Commerce, is organized into trade development sections specializing in such industry sectors as capital goods, consumer goods, transportation, and industrial goods and services. Its staff includes experts on every country in the world including communist nations. The International Trade Administration offers assistance ranging from export mailing lists to product marketing services.

The United States and Foreign Commercial Service is an arm of the International Trade Administration. It was created to help American exports by assisting American businesses.

The Department of Commerce

The Department of Commerce has a marketing manager for Thailand who assists American firms with information and strategies for marketing in Thailand. Commerce publishes *Market Share Reports* which describe overseas markets. Its Office of Major Contracts assists U.S. firms in obtaining large foreign contracts. *World Data Reports* provides credit information on about two hundred thousand foreign firms. Statistical data on trade with Thailand is documented in reports titled *United States Trade With Major Trading Partners.*

The Agency for International Development

The Agency for International Development provides feasibility funding for trade contracts and investments abroad. It also funds banks which finance joint American and foreign ventures.

The Export-Import Bank

The Export-Import Bank develops America's export potential by encouraging small and medium-sized businesses to export goods and services. It offers an array of loans, guarantees, and insurance programs. The Foreign Credit Insurance Corporation acts as an agent for the Export-Import Bank to insure American exporters against non-payment by foreign buyers.

The Overseas Private Investment Corporation

The Overseas Private Investment Corporation is the key federal agency for encouragement of American business investment in developing nations. It furnishes feasibility funding, sponsors investment and trade missions, and provides insurance for currency convertibility, expropriation, war, and revolution. Direct loans and guarantees are also available. This corporation publishes a 270 page reference manual titled *Washington's Best Kept Secrets: A U.S. Guide To International Business.*

The Small Business Administration

The Small Business Administration guarantees export financing and is structured to meet the needs of the small business owner who plans to enter export markets for the first time. The SBA operates both management and financial assistance programs. It helps connect American exporters with foreign buyers.

The State Department

The State Department publishes bulletins which provide market leads. State's Office of Business and Export Affairs publishes information on strategies and risk evaluation for American businesses considering foreign operations.

U.S. Embassy in Thailand

The U.S. Embassy in Bangkok is an excellent source of help. The U.S. Trade Representative provides feasibility study funding for trade, contracts, and investment in Thailand. It also publishes information on commercial treaties and trade problems. The Foreign Commercial Service provides industry analyses, counsels American businesses, and provides financial information on Thai businesses including potential business partners. The economic section provides information on the Thai economy. The Foreign Agricultural Service furnishes information on Thai agriculture and forestry.

Local Government Agencies

More and more states, counties, and cities are developing programs designed to assist firms in international business. Many state and local governments now sponsor trade missions to Thailand.

PRIVATE AMERICAN ORGANIZATIONS

Dun and Bradstreet

Dun and Bradstreet issues *Private International Businesses* which lists credit information on fifty thousand firms in over a hundred nations.

U.S. Attorneys Specializing in Foreign Law

A list of attorneys who specialize in foreign law may be obtained from the International Trade Administration, Department of Commerce.

Chamber of Commerce

The American Chamber of Commerce in Thailand is well situated to help American business. This experienced and competent organization publishes comprehensive up-to-date material on Thai business conditions, laws, and practices. American companies starting to do business in Thailand should consider early contact and membership.

American Banks

American banks, such as Chase Manhattan and Bank of America, have branches in Thailand. These local offices can provide a multitude of services and advice. They are well aware of local business conditions.

Trading Companies

A 1982 American law allowing the formation of trading companies benefits small and medium-sized companies wishing to trade abroad. Check your attorney; under certain conditions firms can join together to form trading companies. Some provisions of U.S. antitrust laws may be nullified for the purposes of trading companies. The International Trade Administration provides information on ways to obtain exemptions from federal and state antitrust laws and will provide assistance in locating other firms interested in forming trading companies. BankAmerica World Trade Corporation is an example of a trading company in action. It offers a full range of services, including export, import, third country, and countertrade transactions. This company will take title to goods and act as a broker or joint-venture partner. Other services relate to international transportation, insurance, and finance. A staff of area and product specialists provides expertise for international transactions.

Training Programs

There are some excellent short programs designed to prepare American executives for the cultural and business challenges of Thailand. Prominent among these are BCIU at American University in Washington, D.C., and Business Programs of the East-West Center in Honolulu.

There is also help for language problems. The Pacific International Language School in Honolulu offers short courses in Thai and operates an Asian branch in Tokyo. Many American corporations send executives bound for Asia to Hawaii for language training en route.

The computer can be an effective tool for language learning and translation. Pacific Rim Connections in Burlingame, California, is an excellent source for Asian language software, including Thai.

Relocation and Orientation Companies

Pacific Rim Connections also offers help in relocation, cultural adjustment, and living in Asia. VLM Enterprises of Wilmington, Delaware, a pioneer in relocation to Asia, publishes *Moving Abroad*, a definitive work on the relocation process. International Orientation Services of Northbrook, Illinois, has one of the best qualified staffs in the business. The main professional organization for intercultural education, training, and research is SIETAR International based in Washington, D.C. The author is a member and recommends its wide variety of services.

THAI ORGANIZATIONS

Thai Government Agencies

The Board of Investment of Thailand is the central coordinating agency for the Thai government organizations described in Chapter Seven. The Royal Thai Embassy in Washington, D.C., and Thai consulates are important sources of information.

Upon request the Ministry of Industry will send the following pamphlets: "Industrial Development in Thailand," "The Image of Thai Industry in the 1990s," "The Investment Environment in Thailand," and "Factors Contributing to Industrial Development." The Board of Investment will send "Thailand Business Legal Handbook" and "Manufacturing for Export in Thailand." These publications should be used as basic guides for information on Thai business law, policies and regulations. They are more detailed and timely than excerpts from them contained in this book.

Thai Businesses

Several Thai businesses can provide help. The most notable in the field of cross-cultural management is Cross-Cultural Management of Thailand, which offers monthly seminars involving both Thai and American employees. Community Services of Bangkok offers excellent orientation and counseling services.

Thai Organizations in the United States

Thai communities in the United States usually have close connections with their counterparts in Thailand. Many of these organizations are listed in your local yellow pages. They can be dependable sources of information and contacts.

Part Three

Thailand: The Personal Experience

This book is not intended to be a tourist guide, but this section should increase your enjoyment of Thailand.

There will be considerable overlap between your personal and business activities. Your adjustment to Thailand and your understanding of its people will enhance your business effectiveness.

The more you enjoy Thailand and its people the greater success you will have in your business endeavors.

10. Travel Tips

Passports and Visas

A U.S. passport is required to enter Thailand. Applications for U.S. passports can be made at designated post offices. No visa is needed for U.S. citizens to enter Thailand for a maximum of fifteen days. Transit visas permit thirty-day stays; tourist visas, sixty days; non-immigrant visas, ninety days. Permission of the Immigration Division is required for stays over ninety days. Since tourist visas may not be renewed, business visitors prefer the flexibility of non-immigrant visas. A photocopy of a confirmed onward ticket must be submitted with the visa application. Thai visas must be used within ninety days of issuance. No inoculations or vaccinations are required unless entering Thailand from an infected area.

One should contact the Royal Thai Embassy or consulates for application forms and possible changes in requirements. Addresses are listed in Chapter Thirteen.

Airports and Hotels

Bangkok is the major hub for international air traffic. Over thirty airlines offer frequent flights to major world cities. Phuket and Chiang Mai offer flights to other cities in Southeast Asia.

Bangkok has two main hotel areas. The first, on the east bank of the Chao Phaya River, is the old tourist section. Here are the Oriental Hotel, the Royal Orchid, Sheraton, and Shangri-la. The Oriental has suites dedicated to former guests: Joseph Conrad, Somerset Maugham, Graham Greene. The east bank hotels are best if you are doing business in Thonburi. The second major hotel section is about five miles inland from the river. It includes downtown hotels such as the Regent Bangkok, Hilton International, and Siam International. You will need to choose a hotel near your place of business because ubiquitous traffic jams will impede your movement around town. A representative list of hotels is included in Chapter Thirteen.

Timing the Visit

The heat in Thailand lessens slightly from January through March. Be prepared for heat at other times. My plane landed in Bangkok at midnight in early December; it was eighty-two degrees.

Packing

For business purposes pressed cotton or linen trousers, shirt and tie are standard. A jacket may be in order for more formal meetings or evening engagements. One will be able to wear a suit only in air-conditioned hotels or offices. One should avoid clothes which are made of synthetic material or are too abbreviated, except at resort or beach areas. Bring a reliable umbrella and a sweater if you plan to visit the northern part of Thailand.

Frequent business travelers pack favorite items such as small sewing and first-aid kits, folding hangers for steaming away wrinkles over a bathtub, dental floss, gift-wrapping paper, vitamins, toilet tissue, insect repellent, cold remedies, and small digital alarm clocks.

Departure from the United States

It is best not to exchange substantial amounts of dollars into Thai baht at your U.S. departure point. Banks and moneychangers in Thailand offer better rates. Take small denominations of dollars and traveler's checks for use until money can be exchanged in Thailand. American Express, Visa, MasterCard, and other major credit cards are honored widely in Thailand. But be sure to carry baht if you visit the north or rural areas. One should obtain a receipt for dollars exchanged for baht to facilitate exchange of baht for dollars on departure.

Duty-free shops at U.S. departure airports and aboard planes over the Pacific offer bargain prices. This is a good time to buy business gifts for your Thai counterparts. The same items at Asian airports are often highly priced. It is a good idea to pack some gift paper and tape since wrapping services are not always convenient. Be sure to register the serial numbers of your foreign-made possessions with U.S. Customs at the departure airport, so you will not have to pay duty on these items upon your return to the United States.

En Route

Your trip to Thailand from the United States will take at least seventeen hours and involve at least one stop. You will lose a day on your westward flight, but gain it back on your return. When it is noon Monday in California, it is 3:00 A.M. Tuesday in Thailand. Your air ticket and travel agency itinerary will refer to local times. You can alleviate jet lag by reducing your intake of food, alcohol, and caffeine while en route. Drink plenty of water and fruit juice to compensate for the dry air at high altitudes.

Arrival

Don Muang Airport is about twelve miles from Bangkok. Hotel cars, taxis, and bus service are available at the airport. Due to congested traffic the trip from the airport to downtown can take as long as two hours so try to avoid arriving during rush hours. At the time of this writing taxis from the airport to town, arranged through the airport taxi desk, cost about fifteen dollars; Thai Airways mini-vans, about seven dollars per person.

The following items can be brought into Thailand duty-free: one liter of an alcoholic beverage, two hundred cigarettes or 250 grams of cigars or smoking tobacco (per adult); one movie or still camera with three rolls of movie film or five rolls of still film; clothes and toilet articles for personal use. There are special requirements for import cars, firearms, animals, and certain plants. Lists are available from Thai consulates. There are no limitations on the import of traveler's checks or U.S. dollars but amounts over $10,000 must be declared on arrival. One may enter Thailand with a limit of two thousand baht and leave with a limit of five hundred baht.

It is best to reserve a day or two to overcome jet lag. You may feel tired, ill, or out of sorts. Your body's time clock will go awry. You will be disoriented, irritable, and upset; sleepy by day and awake at night. This will be no time for you to hold a business meeting. It may be best to let your Thai counterparts know you have arrived only after you have recovered from jet lag, especially if you are there to negotiate a deal.

Minimizing Costs

Hotels and many restaurants add service charges, so it is easy to tip twice. A tip of ten to fifteen per cent is appropriate at a restaurant with no service charge. Fifty cents per bag is appropriate for porters. Cabbies need not be tipped when fares are negotiated. As in the United States, carry small bills for cabbies who "have no change."

Sending purchases or business items from Thailand to the United States by air can be quite expensive so check the rates. You can save money on long international phone conversations by making them from a nearby overseas telephone office because hotel phone charges can mount up quickly.

The best way to reduce costs and ensure your safety is to avoid being cheated, pickpocketed, or robbed. Never let anyone hold your credit cards longer than necessary; destroy the carbons; carry traveler's checks and use the hotel safe for valuables. One might use a money belt in crowded areas. In recent years gangs operating in Thailand have lured visitors and murdered them with poison or injections to simulate heart attacks to ensure stolen traveler's checks, credit cards and passports would go unreported.

Electricity

Except for a few luxury hotels, all electrical outlets in Thailand run on 220 volts, 50 cycles, alternating current, so bring a transformer and adapter for your 110 volt appliances.

Getting Around

Thailand has adequate rail, boat, and bus transportation. They are efficient and reasonably priced. But during the busy season, January through March, reservations should be made well in advance. Some bus drivers are paid bonuses for beating the schedules, so be prepared for "white knuckle" rides. Some Westerners avoid rental cars due to liability problems.

Business hours are usually eight to five Monday through Friday; some have Saturday morning hours. Banks are open from 8:30 A.M. to 3:30 P.M. Government offices are open from 8:30 A.M. to noon and 1:00 to 4:30 P.M. Most shops do business from 10:00 A.M. to 7:00 P.M. Monday through Saturday; some are open on Sundays.

Bangkok's traffic problems are notorious. It sometimes takes an hour to drive three blocks. A German machinery salesman told me he solved this problem by choosing a hotel within a block or two of his next morning's appointment. Sometimes he moved every night to be near his next morning's business. When entering a cab, he always had his destination and return address written in Thai. Three appointments per day seemed to be the limit.

Bangkok taxis, though air-conditioned, lack meters. Negotiate the fare, based on distance, before entering. The Oriental,one of Bangkok's top hotel's, has Mercedes with car phones for guests. *Tuk-tuks*, a type of rickshaw, are very inexpensive and useful for short trips.

Health Precautions

It is always a good idea to keep your shots current. With an international inoculation record (yellow booklet) showing up-to-date shots for cholera, yellow fever, typhoid, tetanus, plague, and polio, you can go anywhere anytime. Gamma globulin is also available for hepatitis. Until recently there had been a malaria preventative for only three of the four types of malaria; the fourth was resistant. This problem has been removed by the development of mefloquinine which covers all malaria. It is best to contact your health professional regarding inoculations. Some series must begin months in advance of your departure.

Other health precautions are standard for most of Asia. Do not drink tap water, only boiled or bottled. Do not eat peeled fruit or vegetables unless they have been washed with purified or boiled water. Adjust to the tropics by respecting the sun, drinking lots of bottled water, and avoiding too much exertion and alcohol. Do not swim in polluted water.

Departure and Return

Your airline will want you to report to the airport several hours early. There is a departure tax of two hundred baht (about eight dollars) for international flights.

Certain categories of aliens must obtain a Tax Clearance Certificate within fifteen days of leaving Thailand: those who visit Thailand for work or business, those who hold a Thai Certificate of Residence, those with non-immigrant category "B" visas who stay more than fourteen days, and those who stay more than ninety consecutive days or ninety days per year.

When you return to the United States, Customs will allow you to bring in four hundred dollars worth of goods duty-free. If you have stayed outside the United States over thirty-one days this total increases. If you exceed the limit, you will have to pay a ten per cent duty on the first thousand dollars of excess over the four hundred dollar exemption. At this point it gets more complicated; it is best to check with Customs if you plan extensive purchases. Write the U.S. Customs Service for information regarding the General System of Preferences. For purchases over $250 be sure to get a certificate of origin showing the country of purchase and the amount paid. There is an IRS tax on liquor over one bottle. Articles purchased abroad and mailed to the United States are subject to a duty if valued at fifty dollars or more. It is a good idea to pack your purchases in a separate suitcase to avoid delay at Customs.

11. Living in Thailand

Moving and Arrival

Your move to Thailand will be a major project. Many American firms will hire a relocation company to process travel documents, ship household goods, find housing, and arrange school enrollment for children. A good relocation company can sometimes save considerably more than it costs.

If you are planning to live in Thailand, rather than just visit, the customs requirements get complicated. Autos may be brought into Thailand with a vehicle registration, driver's license, and suitable cash or bank guarantees. Firearms and ammunition can only be imported with a permit from the Thai police. Permits for entry of pets are available at the airport for air arrival; by sea, in advance from the Department of Livestock Development in Bangkok. Proof of inoculations for pets is required. The Department of Agriculture controls the import of plants.

Many of the modern products produced in Thailand are sold only on export markets. It may be difficult to find specialized items on the local market. So bring along a supply of favorite items such as books, medicines, pens and cartridges, cosmetics, toiletries, spices, cooking utensils, fireplace screens, and bathroom scales. Thailand uses the metric system so bring your own items of measurement for English measures to be used for recipes and weather temperature. An alternative is to adjust to the metric system. One meter equals 1.09 yards, about 39 inches. One kilometer is roughly two-thirds of a mile. One liter equals 1.06 quarts or .26 gallons. One kilogram equals 2.2 pounds.

Do not pack for shipment items you will need during your trip and while waiting for your goods. While you are settling your finances, save some time to check your car, house, and health insurance, cancel utilities, and obtain an international driver's license. An excellent book on foreign relocation is *Moving Abroad: A Guide to International Living* by Virginia McKay published in Wilmington, Delaware.

Most companies assign someone to help new arrivals clear customs. It is a good idea to register your name and address at the U.S. Embassy in Bangkok soon after your arrival in Thailand.

Cultural Shock

You will not suffer from cultural shock immediately upon your arrival in Thailand; it takes awhile to get the disease. The symptoms will appear when you realize you are not a tourist but someone who will have to live as a foreigner in a strange environment. As soon as your initial enthusiasm for everything Thai wears off, you will feel considerable frustration and irritation due to difficulties with food, weather, customs, language, and manners. You may give up and go home.

Your business success will depend largely on your personal adjustment. To contribute to your company's Thai venture, you will have to break out of your Western shell. To become your firm's Thai expert, you will have to learn something about Thai culture, economy, politics, and language. How can this be done?

There are many Thai language schools in Thailand. The American University Alumni Association is said to offer the best courses. The monthly seminars conducted by Cross-Cultural Management are designed to help Westerners function in a Thai business environment. Community Services of Bangkok helps overcome cultural shock in at least two ways. It offers Western-trained counselors to help expatriate individuals and families. It also serves as a social center where expatriates can meet each other. Activities include events, clubs, cooking classes, and help in getting settled.

Housing and Schools

There are many considerations in finding housing besides rental costs. What will electrical and phone services cost? Is there a community guard system? Are groceries and foreign schools convenient? Is school bus service available? Is a car needed? Are taxis and buses nearby? Does the building have storage room and an emergency water supply? How far is it from the airport?

Most foreigners live in the Sukhumvit Road area, close to businesses, shopping, and Bangkok's International School. Rental costs range from about $1200 per month to $2000 with some as high as $3200. Most rentals are fully or partly furnished. Utilities are extra. Many expatriates bring their clothes washers and dryers, refrigerators, and dishwashers since these cost more in Thailand than in the United States. Houses can be rented through newspaper ads, relocation companies, or rental agencies.

The International School offers instruction from kindergarten through the twelfth grade.

Household Servants

Most expatriates will employ one or more servants such as maids, cooks, gardeners, guards, or drivers. Some servants may be shared with neighbors. Families with several children will often have more than one maid. A live-in servant will help prevent theft of your possessions. Salaries are based on experience and range from $120 to $240 per month. Probably the best way to obtain a household servant is from another Westerner who is returning to the United States. Then you will likely get an employee who is honest, reliable, and trained in Western ways. Such matters as salary reviews, bonuses, health exams, room and board, holidays, vacations, and termination pay should be settled at the time of hiring.

Since most Americans are not accustomed to having servants, the experience can be difficult. If you putter around in the kitchen, it will be taken as an invasion of the cook's domain. Your servants will tend to violate your privacy and spoil your children.

Radio and Television

There is considerable English-language programming in Thailand. American Armed Forces Radio and BBC can be received. Thai television stations broadcast American programs dubbed in Thai, but the English soundtrack is available simultaneously on FM. Electrical outlets are 220 volts, 50 cycles, A.C., so bring a transformer and an adapter.

Postal, Telephone, Telex

Thailand has an excellent postal system. Before you have an address, you can have mail addressed to you at Post Restante (General Delivery). There is a Postal Restante window at the main post office in each city. Federal Express also operates in Thailand.

There are Post, Telephone, and Telegraph Offices (called PTT) open twenty-four hours a day in most cities; they accept both credit card and collect calls. FAX service is available at many hotels. Public telephones are colored red.

Newspapers

The Bangkok Post, a daily, publishes in English. It produces a good balance of international and domestic news. *The Nation,* another English daily, sometimes includes a tourist magazine, *Saen Sanuk. USA Today, The Asian Wall Street Journal,* and *The International Herald Tribune* are sold on newsstands.

Health Problems

Thailand has many health problems although conditions in Bangkok are better than the countryside. A big malarial eradication program was effective; yet the disease is still endemic in much of the nation. Especially when outside of Bangkok be sure to use mosquito netting, insect repellent, and wear long sleeves at night. Check with your health professional about the new malaria preventative.

More than half of all Thai people suffer from intestinal parasites. The high-water table of Bangkok is polluted and limited pumping capacity sometimes creates a suction in peak usage which sucks groundwater into the pipes. It only makes sense to drink bottled or boiled water.

Other health problems include tuberculosis, leprosy, hepatitis, trachoma, salmonella, liver flukes, and rabies. Rabies has been difficult to control due to Buddhist restrictions on killing dogs. Cholera, once prevalent, is now rare. Eat only fruits and vegetables and use only eating utensils which have been washed in treated water. Take care with raw seafood, pastries, and salads; food hot off the wok is much safer. Avoid walking barefoot or swimming in polluted water.

A wise person once said, "Travel broadens the mind and loosens the bowels." One-third of all visitors to Thailand get diarrhea, so ask your health professional about Imodium and Septra.

Thailand has a modern medical system with trained surgeons, physicians, and dentists. It has excellent hospitals. The U.S. Embassy publishes a list of recommended health professionals.

Reverse Cultural Shock

You will likely experience reverse cultural shock upon your return to the United States. This might be severe if there has been substantial social change during your absence. My family and I were in Asia during the American cultural revolution of the 1960s. We returned to the United States of the 1970s with 1950s habits, ideas, and values, strangers in our own land.

American values, social movements, politics, habits, and speech are probably the most dynamic in the world. If you keep track of recent developments by reading American news magazines and talking with newly arrived Americans, you will lessen the impact of reverse cultural shock upon your return to the United States.

12. Things to Do, See and Learn

A New Perspective

Although this is not intended to be a tourist guidebook, information on things to do, see, and learn are included because your ability to understand and enjoy Thailand will have a direct impact on your business efficiency. As you become knowledgeable of Thailand, your Thai counterpart will have more respect for you. Your first-hand experience with Thai society and culture will also give you a fresh perspective on your own. You will enjoy immense opportunities for both personal and business growth.

Bangkok

Bangkok, *Krung Thep*, "the City of Angels," is a logical place to start your exploration of Thailand. It is a study in contrasts. Sleek steel and glass buildings reflect the polished marble and golden spires of ancient wats. In ultramodern hotels silk-clad dancers portray a classical heritage while the streets just outside are congested with noisy, polluting traffic. The city's construction boom raises spirits as well as dust; a place on the roof of each new commercial building is reserved for a prayer house to hold and appease the displaced spirits of the land below. Along the still backwaters of the klongs, immobile fishermen, numb to the modern madness, wait patiently for nibbles.

The city has over four hundred wats and a wide variety of likenesses of Buddha. The Temple of the Golden Buddha contains a priceless five-and-one-half-ton statue discovered in an abandoned monastery in 1953. In the Temple of the Reclining Buddha, the figure supports its huge head on one hand. A thirty-one inch Buddha statue carved from lustrous green jasper is enshrined in the Temple of the Emerald Buddha; the King of Thailand regularly changes its gem-bedaubed garments.

The Rose Garden with its Thai village offers traditional sights and experiences: rumbling elephant rides (whoever invents a shock absorber will make a fortune); Thai boxing, dancing, and dueling. Other popular Bangkok tourist sights include the Grand Palace (with Coronation Hall, Funeral Hall, Harem Building, and Holy Water Pavilion), the National Museum (history, art, and archeology), the City Pillar (installed by Rama I), The Palace of the Cabbage Garden, Red Cross Snake Farm (supplied with antidotes for tourists who tease the cobras, vipers, and kraits), Dusit Zoo, and Celestial Residence.

The South

Scenic pearls south of Bangkok include the beach resort of Pattaya and Phuket, Thailand's largest island. Both are meccas for modern sun worshippers. These coastal areas were once havens for pirates; they have been replaced by marauders out to pillage credit cards and traveler's checks.

The Far North

Thailand's far north, only an hour from Bangkok by air, features the famous Golden Triangle and the city of Chiang Mai, "the rose of the north." Here elephant caravans once plied the ancient trade routes along the cool foothills of the Himalayas; some of their progeny still pull teak trees from the forests. Chiang Mai's old city, moated ruins, is surrounded by worn walls pierced by five gates, each with an exotic name such as White Elephant Gate. Before air conditioning relief from the heat was available only in the north. It took weeks of travel by boat and elephant to escape the soupy swelter of the southern plains.

Near Chiang Mai stone serpents guard the three hundred steps which lead up Suthep Mountain to a view of an immense wilderness.

While most of the Golden Triangle is across the border in Burma and Laos, it includes the ancient Thai cities of Chiang Rai, Lamphun, and Mae Hong Son. But beware! Some 150,000 square miles of poppy fields tend to attract unsavory characters. Every few years some macho Western adventurers set out to explore the vast, primeval, orchid-encrusted north, places of mystery "where no man has gone before." Once out of sight of civilization they vanish forever, perhaps victims of "tour guides" after their credit cards or paranoiac poppy protectors!

Indeed, Thailand's teeming forests conceal many secrets. In places ornate corncob towers rise above the savage majesty of the jungle. These rock wats, now so tightly embraced by roots and vines, were once the spiritual centers of ancient wooden cities, some more populous than Nero's Rome. Now only these temples survive, silent and time-locked, haunting sentinels for long-dead civilizations which once throbbed with life.

Central Thailand

Central Thailand consists of a huge steaming rice-raising plain, a well-watered land washed by numerous rivers, the source of much of the nation's wealth. On the way to Chiang Mai consider an overnight stop at Phitsanulok to see nearby Sukhothai, Thailand's first capital. Here along the banks of the Yom River, amid water buffalo, mango groves, and paddy rice, the Thai culture crystallized. I have always been fascinated by such cradles of civilization as Sukhothai, Indonesia's Borobudur, and Cambodia's Angkor Wat. In each the soul of a people emerged from darkness to shape its unique identity and destiny. So one night I waited alone in the eerie ruins of Sukhothai. At dawn an epiphanous sun emerged from the jungle, baking the skeletal bones of the ancient city in bright scarlet stripes.

Bangkok's Environs

There are several excellent day excursions from Bangkok. A full-day tour includes a speedboat ride to the floating gardens of Damnern Saduk and the Rose Garden Resort. Another involves a visit to the old ruins of the ancient capital of Ayuttaya. By riding the bus upriver and the boat back, you will be on the cooler river during the hot afternoon. Ayuttaya is about forty-five miles north of Bangkok. Years ago it was completely destroyed by invading Burmese during a long siege. Most of Thailand's historical and literary records burned in the flames.

It is even possible to see the bridge on the River Kwai. It can be visited on a day trip but it is better to stay overnight in the nearby town of Kanchanaburi. Although this area was no fun for the prisoners forced to build the bridge and railroad, you will enjoy its scenic rivers, cool waterfalls, and misty mountains.

Dining

Thailand has such a variety of fine food that you will want to dine out often. Addresses of interesting restaurants are listed in Chapter Thirteen.

Thai food, hot, pungent, and spicy, brings tears to the eyes and water to the tongue; the first Thai phrase you must learn is "mai ped," meaning "not hot." The Thai prefer sticky, glutinous rice, which is often pressed into balls placed in the center of the table as devices to scoop up other food.

Thai food, like Chinese, is usually stir fried in woks, but Thai cuisine is unique, not a variant of Chinese cooking. Coconut milk is often a key ingredient; this is not the liquid readily found in a coconut, but a liquid squeezed from the meat after soaking it in boiling milk or water. Thai food involves Indian spices and a great variety of noodles and rice. A wide range of curries are concocted with such spices as garlic, chili, and coriander. Unlike the Chinese and Vietnamese, Thais do not eat dogs.

A meal often begins with *Kong Tan Lin*, a variety of appetizers. *Tom Yam Gung,* Thailand's favorite soup, is clear, sour, and spicy, featuring prawns flavored with chili, lime leaves, lemon grass, and coriander leaves. *Tom Yam Gai,* chicken and coconut soup, is almost as popular.

Typical main courses include sizzling sticks of *Satay,* strips of skewered beef, chicken, or pork dipped in a sauce of peanuts, coconut, and curry; *Larb,* spicy ground beef or chicken with mint or lime; and various dishes of chicken: *Gai Sawan,* delicately flavored in heaven; *Gai Tord,* dipped in pungent *Nam Prik* sauce; *Gai Hoa Bai,* wrapped in leaves and fried. Everyone likes *Mee Krob,* crisp fried rice noodles flecked with chicken and shrimp.

Seafood courses include *Pla Brio Wan*, whole fish sauced with soy and ginger; *Tot Mun Goong,* shrimp cakes; and *Tot Mun Pla,* a spicy fish dish.

For deserts Thai cooks often rely on delicious fruits: mangoes, pineapples, guavas, papayas, purple mangosteens, watermelons, durians, and coconuts. These are sometimes supplemented with chilled lichees in custard, or candied bananas dipped in caramel and specked with sesame seeds.

Thais like beer: Singha beer is very fine; Amarit, better; Kloster, best. Most wines are imported and very expensive. Mekhong is the local hard liquor.

Shopping

For a shopper Thailand offers a pirate's treasure: exotic lacquer ware, slick silk, fine celadon, teak artifacts, precious works in jewels, silver, and gold. A river *hang yao* can slip you into narrow klongs filled with floating shops. The Damnern Saduk, a bobbing market of rafts and boats some forty miles from Bangkok, offers handicrafts at bargain prices.

Gems are a key attraction: star sapphires, Burmese rubies, South Sea pearls. Jewelry involving considerable hand labor in its production can be a bargain.

For Thai silks visit the Jim Thompson Store at 9 Surawong Road in Bangkok. Jim is not there anymore; the wealthy silk magnate was last seen in Malaysia in 1967.

But buyer beware! In Thailand there are so many fake products they are graded by quality!

If you plan to be in Thailand for only a few days or weeks and want to buy tailored clothing, you should make arrangements immediately after arrival because several fittings are needed. Prices are by far the lowest in Asia.

There are some excellent antiques for sale in Bangkok, but antique statues of Buddha cannot be taken out of Thailand.

Bargaining

Except in the very best stores, bargaining is expected. Before bargaining visit a variety of shops, such as those in Thewarat Market; Sukhumvit Road, and Bangkok Market to get an idea of prices. Stay well below the asking price. Be sure to bargain in good humor. Some shoppers prefer to visit shops listed in *The Official Shopping Guide.*

Spectator Sports

There are many spectator sports available in Thailand. Horse races are held weekends in Bangkok at either the Royal Bangkok Sports Club or the Royal Turf Club.

The main interest many Thais have in sports is the opportunity to gamble. They wage on fights between cocks, bulls, fish, and crickets, also on Western sports such as soccer. There are no matadors in Thai bullfights; instead they feature two bulls.

Be sure to see a Thai boxing match. Before the contest both boxers kneel and pray for help from the Spirit of the Ring. Usually they need it. A Thai boxer may legally kick, knee, or elbow an opponent on *any* part of his body. However, it is against the rules to bite or kick an opponent *while he is down.*

Participant Sports

Bangkok offers badminton, tennis, and golf. Bangkok has five golf courses including the Royal Thai Air Force links which are laid out between the runways of Don Muang Airport. There are also golf courses in Phuket,

Pattaya, Hua Hin, Nakhorn Pathom, and Chiang Mai; so bring your sticks!

Most hotels have swimming pools, and there are many public beaches.

Some rural Thais still consider working up a sweat to be a sign of low status. They do not understand the difference between working and working out. If they see you in hard exercise (in tennis, for example), they may offer to do "the work" for you!

Performing Arts

Most Thai still like *sanuk,* entertainment films like soap operas based on such themes as love triangles and family crises. These usually last for a minimum of two hours because viewers expect to enjoy theater air conditioning that long.

Only in the past few years have Thai films involved social commentary. Prince Chatri's *The Elephant Keeper* deals with illegal logging. Jazz Siam's *Silhouette of God* weaves a tale of a farmer who becomes a medium. Both reflect a new style for Thai films.

Thai classical dance with its subtle movements is known all over the world. In Bangkok there are often free performances of Thai classical dances at Lak Muang Shrine and Bahmin God Shrine, sometimes at the National Theater. Some restaurants and hotels offer shows with a Thai meal.

Seree Vangnaitham is widely recognized as "the diamond of Thai performing arts." For more than thirty years this actor, musician, composer, vocalist, and playwright has regaled audiences. If you have an opportunity to see a performance of one of his drama, musical, or dance performances do not miss it.

At public performances the audience can be almost as interesting as the performers. Thai like to eat and talk at public entertainment productions. Although it is now changing, it has been taboo in Thai tradition for people of the opposite sex to affectionately touch each other in public. But people of the same sex routinely do so with no implications of homosexuality. A newspaper photo of a general and a cabinet minister holding hands at a play would raise no eyebrows.

Night Life

Some of the most popular evening events are the classical music and dance demonstrations held at the National Theater and major restaurants.

There are many nightclubs and discos. Those at major hotels are considered best. Bangkok has a full range of bars, from quiet serene elegance to blasting bands. The city's notorious sin zones, such as Patpong Road, are anachronistic vestiges of the Vietnam War era. Though the millions of American troops who visited here in the 1960s are now approaching retirement years, these sexual theme parks, each with its array of V.D. clinics, strip joints, and gay bars, remain. Raucous, raunchy, and rowdy, their clatter contrasts with the silent insidious work of the AIDS virus.

I was never able to find out why Thailand, a devoutly Buddhist nation, should be a sexual magnet. I did discover that this country has many more monks than prostitutes: something to think about.

13. Useful Addresses

This chapter lists useful addresses and phone numbers. The purpose of this list is to help you get started. No attempt is made to include all addresses in a category. Listed hotels and restaurants should be suitable for business purposes. Thai telephone directories are available by mail from the American Embassy, U.S. & Foreign Commercial Service, Bangkok.

Accounting Firms

Arthur Andersen & Co.
514/1 Lamluang
Bangkok 280-0900

Bunchikiji Co. Ltd
1126/1 New Phetburi
Bangkok 250-1067

Attorneys

Ukrit Mongkolnavin Law Offices
10 Soi 5 Sukhumvit
Bangkok 252-6080/2

International Legal Counsellors, Ltd.
Kaplan, Russin, & Vecchi
Bangkok Bank Bldg. - 18th Floor
333 Silom Road, Bangkok 10500
234-0230 235-0780

Krisana Law Office
374/14 Soi Petchburi 12
Petchburi Road
Bangkok 215-7851

Banks in Thailand (American)

Bank of America
2/2 Wireless Road
Bangkok 251-6333

Citibank
127 S. Sathorn Road
Bangkok 213-2441

Chase Manhattan Bank
Siam Center
965 Rama 1 Road
Bangkok 252-1141

Security Pacific Asian Bank
313 Silom Road
Bangkok 231-0320

Business Training Programs

American Graduate School of
International Management
Glendale, Arizona 85306
(602) 978-7011

Business Training & Development
Institute (BCIU)
Executive Programs - Suite 244
The American University
3301 New Mexico Avenue
Washington, D.C. 20016
(202) 686-2771

PA Management Consultants
120 Silom Road
Bangkok 233-9558

Business Programs
East-West Center
1777 East-West Road
Honolulu, Hawaii 96848
(808) 944-7611

Cross-Cultural Management
Wijai Wattanaham Ltd.
62 Sukhumvit Soi 26
Bangkok 258-4928 391-5391

Global Dynamics
6 Senaca Trail
Randolph, NJ 07869
(201) 927-9135

Car Rentals - Bangkok

Avis-Bangkok
233-0397
(Offices throughout Thailand)

Hertz - Bangkok
253-6251
(Offices throughout Thailand)

Chambers of Commerce

American Chamber of Commerce
in Thailand
7th Floor, Shell House
140 Wireless Road
Bangkok 251-9266 251-1605

The Thai Chamber of Commerce
150 Rajbopit Road
Bangkok 221-3351 221-6532

Hospitals

Bangkok General Hospital
2 Soi Soonvijai 7
New Petchburi Road
Bangkok 318-0066

Kluaynawitai Hospital
80 Soi Kluaynawitai
Rama IV
Bangkok 381-2006

St. Louis Hospital
215 Sathorn Thai Road
Yannawa, Bangkok
212-0033-48

Sukhumvit Hospital
1411 Sukhamvit Road
Bangkok 391-0011

Hotels - Bangkok

(Luxury)

The Oriental
48 Soi Burapa New Road
236-0400

Hilton International
2 Wireless Road
253-0123

Regent of Bangkok
155 Ratchadamri Rd.
251-6127

Shangri-la Hotel
89 Soi Wat Suan Plu
236-7777

(First Class)

Meridien President
135-26 Gaysorn Road
253-0444

The Mandarin
662 Rama IV Road
233-5370

Royal Orchid Sheraton
2 Soi Captain Bush Lane
234-5599

Tawana Hotel
80 Surawong Road
236-0361

(Moderate)

New Fuji
299-301 Surawong Road
234-5364

Victory Hotel
322 Silom Road
233-9060

Hotels - Outside Bangkok

Amarintr Nakorn
3/1 Chao Phrya Road
Phitsanulok
(055) 258-586

Royal Cliff Beach Resort
Royal Wing is luxury
Pattaya
(038) 421-421

Hotel Suriwongse
110 Chang Klan Road
Chiang Mai
(053) 236-733

President
226 Vichayanon Road
Chiang Mai
(053) 251-025

Chiang Mai Plaza Hotel
92 Sri Donchai Road
Chiang Mai
(053) 236-733

Novotel Tropicana
45 Beach Road
Pattaya
(038) 428-645

Investment, Industry, and Trade Agencies in Thailand

Alien's Occupation Division
Labour Department
Mitrmaitri Road
Bangkok 245-3902 245-3700

Department of Foreign Trade
Sanamchai Road
Bangkok 223-1481

Ministry of Industry
Rama VI Road
Bangkok 281-6061 246-1137

Office of National Economic and
Social Development Board
962 Krung Kasem Road
Bangkok 282-1151 282-3861

Commercial Registration Dept.
Maharaj Road
Bangkok 221-3865 222 6918

Ministry of Commerce
Sanamchai Road
Bangkok 222-0855

Office of Board of Investment
16th Fl. Farmers Bank Bldg.
400 Phaholyothin Rd.
Bangkok 270-1400 270-1420

Language Services and Training

Nisa Thai Language School
127 Sathorn Tai Road
Bangkok 286-9323

Pacific International Language School
1451 S. King Street-Ste #404
Honolulu, Hawaii 96814
(808) 946-8485

Pacific Rim Connections, Inc.
3030 Atwater Drive
Burlingame, CA 94010
(415) 697-0911
(Asian language software)

Thai Language Courses
American University Alumni Assoc.
179 Rajadamri Road
Bangkok 251-1606/7 252-4021

Physicians

Tha Phra Poly Clinic
2/11-12 Phetkasem Road
Bangkok 466-6184

Yanhee Poly Clinic
9/20 Charansanit Wong
Bangkok 424-0606

Relocation, Consulting, Community Services Companies

Clarke Consulting Group, Inc.
Three Lagoon Drive-Ste #230
Redwood City, CA 94065
(415) 591-8100

Community Services of Bangkok
15 Soi 33 Sukhumvit Road
Bangkok
258-5663 253-2871

International Orientation Resources
707 Skokie Blvd. #350
Northbrook, IL 60062
(312) 205-0066

VLM Enterprises
P.O. Box 7236
Wilmington, DE 19803

Restaurants

(Thai)

Lemon Grass Restaurant
5/1 Soi 24 (off Sukhumvit Road)
Bangkok 258-8637

Bussaracum
35 Soi Pipat 2
(off Silam Road)
Bangkok 235-8915

Sala Thip
Shangri-la Hotel
Bangkok 236-0280

Thanying Restaurant
10 Pramun St.
(near Oriental Hotel)
Bangkok 236-4361

(Other Asian Cuisines)

Edith Tai's Silver Palace
Silom Road & 5 Soi Pipat
Bangkok 235-5118 (Chinese)

Tai Pan
Imperial Hotel
Bangkok 254-0111 (Chinese)

Daikoku
960/1 Rama IV Road
Bangkok 233-1495 (Japanese)

Shang Palace
Shangri-la Hotel
Bangkok 236-0280 (Chinese)

Cafe India
460/8 Suriwongse Road
Bangkok 233-0419 (Indian)

Le Dalat
51 Sukhumvit Soi 23
Bangkok 258-9298 (Vietnamese)

(Western Cuisines)

Ma Maison
Hilton Hotel
Bangkok 236-0400 (French)

Whole Earth Restaurant
93/3 Soi Langsuan
Bangkok 252-5574 (health food)

Pan Pan
Sukhumvit Road & Soi 33
Bangkok 258-9304 (Italian)

Seafood Restuarant
388 Sukhumvit Road
Bangkok 258-0218 (seafood)

Shipping and Express Companies

Federal Express
Room 346, Cargo Terminal #2
Bangkok Intl. Airport
531-2513

United Parcel Service
(picks up)
Bangkok
511-1679 511-2190

Taxis

Bangkok Taxi
Bangkok 424-3062

Nakhomchai Taxi Co.
Bangkok 467-2074

Thai Diplomatic & Information Offices

Royal Thai Embassy
2300 Kalorama Road NW
Washington, D.C. 20008
(202) 234-5052

Royal Thai Consulate-General
801 N. LaBrea Ave.
Los Angeles, CA 90038
(213) 937-1894

Royal Thai Consulate-General
53 Park Place Rooms 505/507
New York, N.Y. 10007
(212) 732-8166

Royal Thai Consulate-General
35 East Wacker Drive Ste. 1834
Chicago, IL 60601
(312) 236-2447/8

Ministry of Foreign Affairs
Saranyom Palace Bldg.
Sanamchai Road
Bangkok 225-0096

Office of Information
4250 Connecticut Ave. NW #26
Washington, D.C.
(202) 667-3108

Thai Immigration

Immigration Division
National Police Department
Soi Suan Piu
Yannawa, Bangkok
286-9230 286-9176

Thai Financial Institutions

Bank of Agriculture and
Agriculture Co-operatives
469 Nakon Sawan Road
Bangkok 282-5770/9

Bank of Thailand
273 Samsen Road
Bangkok 282-3322

Excise Duties Department
Nakornchaisri Road
Bangkok 241-4778

Fiscal Policy Office
Naphralan Road
Bangkok 222-8186/90

Revenue Department
Chakrpong Road
Bangkok 281-5777

Securities Exchange of Thailand
2nd Floor, Sinthon Bldg.
Wireless Road
Bangkok 250-0001/8

Thai Trade Institutions

Thai Trading Center
3440 Wilshire Blvd.
Los Angeles (617) 380-5943

Thai Foreign Trade Department
Sanamchai Road
Bangkok 223-1413/5

Thai Customs Department
Art Narong Road, Klong Toey
Bangkok 286-1010

Thai Export Service Center
22/77 Rachadapisek Road
Bangkok 511-5066/7

Ministry of Industry
Rama 6 Road, Bangkok 10400
246-1137

Board of Investment
555 Vipavadee-Rangsit Road
Bangken, Bangkok 10900
270-1400/10/20

Travel Services

American Express c/o Sea Tours
#414 Siam Center
Bangkok 251-4862
235-0090 or 253-8377 (for lost cards, TCs, etc.)

Major Home Travel Agency Company
120/14 Rajprarop Road
Bangkok 250-1685
255-2609 251-5019

U.S. Embassy

Embassy of the United States
95 Witthayu Road
Bangkok 252-5040/9
(APO San Francisco 96346)

U.S. Government Agencies

Agency for International Development
320 21st St. NW
Washington, D.C. 20523
(202) 663-1451

Center for International Education
U.S. Department of Education
400 Maryland Ave. SW
Washington, D.C. 20202
(202) 732-3283

Department of Agriculture
Foreign Agricultural Service
Independence Ave. btwn. 12th/14th
Washington, D.C. 20250
(202) 447-8732

Department of Commerce
14th St. & Constitution Ave.
Washington, D.C. 20230
(202) 377-4399

Export-Import Bank
811 Vermont Ave. NW
Washington, D.C. 20571
(202) 566-2117

International Trade Administration
14th St. & Constitution Ave.
Washington, D.C. 20230
(202) 377-2000

Overseas Private Investment Corporation
1615 M St. NW
Washington, D.C. 20527
(202) 457-7200

Small Business Administration
Office of International Trade
1441 L Street NW
Washington, D.C. 20416
(202) 634-1500

U.S. & Foreign Commercial Service
14th Street btwn. E St. & Constitution Ave.
Washington, D.C.
(202) 377-2000

14. Additional Reading

Bunge, Frederica M. *Thailand.* Washington, D.C.: U.S. Government Printing Office, 1981.

Chakrabongse, Prince Chula. *Lords of Life.* New York: Taplinger Publishing Company, Inc., 1960. This is a revealing look at Thai life by a Thai prince.

Cordier, C. et. al. *Thailand: Guide to Business and Investment.* Aldershot, U.K: Gower Publishing Company, Ltd., 1986. Good coverage of the Thai business environment.

DeYoung, John E. *Village Life in Modern Thailand.* Berkeley: University of California Press, 1955.

Fieg, John Paul, and Murlock, Liz. *A Common Core: Thais and Americans.* Yarmouth, ME: Intercultural Press, Inc., 1989. A valuable, incisive comparison of Thais and Americans.

Investment in Thailand. Hong Kong: Peat, Marwick, and Mitchell, 1985. Excellent coverage of ways and means of investing in Thailand.

Krairiksh, Piriya. *The Sacred Image.* Bangkok: White Lotus, 1980. A sensitive study of Thai art.

Lewis, Paul and Elaine. *Peoples of the Golden Triangle.* London: Thames and Hudson, 1984. An excellent study of the Thai northern hill tribes.

McKay, Virginia, *Moving Abroad: A Guide to International Living.* Wilmington, DE: VLM Enterprises, 1990. A definitive work on relocation. Order through P.O. Box 7236, Wilmington, DE, 19803.

Phillips, Herbert P. *Thai Peasant Personality: The Patterning of Interpersonal Behavior in the Village of Bang Chan.* Berkeley: University of California Press, 1965.

MAP OF THAILAND

INDEX